# BATTLING HIV/AIDS

## A Decision Maker's Guide to the Procurement of Medicines and Related Supplies

*Yolanda Tayler, Editor*

**THE WORLD BANK**

# Contents

# Boxes

# Figures

# Tables

# Foreword

The HIV/AIDS pandemic has been characterized as the greatest natural challenge ever to confront humanity and one of the great moral causes of our time.

The pandemic is on a rapid global march and is now impacting some of the world's most populous countries. Forty million people worldwide are currently living with the disease and another 45 million may become infected by 2010. The disease is having a particularly devastating impact on Sub-Saharan Africa, where 2.3 million people died of HIV/AIDS in 2003, an estimated 26.6 million people are HIV positive, and there are more than eleven million AIDS orphans. In addition, an estimated five to six million individuals in developing countries are in need of antiretroviral therapy (ART) today.

The world community recognizes that HIV/AIDS is a global priority, and halting and reversing its spread is one of the Millennium Development Goals. The World Bank and other sources of finance, such as the Global Fund to Fight AIDS, Tuberculosis and Malaria and the U.S. Leadership Against HIV/AIDS, Tuberculosis and Malaria Act of 2003 have committed substantial financing to fund HIV/AIDS prevention, care and treatment and mitigation programs. To date the World Bank has committed US$1.6 billion to the war against HIV/AIDS through a combination of grants, loans, and credits, mostly through its Multi-country

HIV/AIDS Programs (MAPs) in Africa and in the Caribbean. Of special importance is providing treatment for the millions of people around the world who are HIV positive and whose lives would be prolonged by the use of anti-retroviral medicines. However, scaling up treatment is a major challenge. The Bank has recognized that waging war against HIV/AIDS means adopting new approaches and procedures.

The Bank's Implementation Acceleration Team was created in January 2003 to—among other things—create solutions wherever existing procedures and practices appeared inadequate for fast and flexible interventions. As a result, significant changes have already been made in a number of areas, such as the implementation of safeguard policies, grant-making authority, knowledge sharing, and financial management, disbursement, and reporting.

This Decision Maker's Guide (hereafter referred to as "the Guide") represents an important further step in this work. While implementing agencies are familiar with how to procure goods and services for traditional development projects, dealing with HIV/AIDS requires new areas of expertise, especially with regard to purchasing antiretroviral medicines and other medical supplies and devices. This Guide on procurement of HIV/AIDS medicines and supplies, which was extensively discussed with and reviewed by stakeholders around the world, is meant as a guide for implementing agencies and donors in these new areas. The Guide adapts the Bank's guidelines on the procurement of health goods to the HIV/AIDS context. In addition, it sets out principles and guidance to ensure that such procurements will fit within an overall well-functioning supply management system for HIV/AIDS medicines and related supplies. Within the contemporary context, this effort requires that attention also be paid to matters such as product selection, quality assurance, and countries' intellectual property rights systems within the global trading system.

The Bank and its partners in the United Nations' Interagency Pharmaceutical Coordination Group are currently working to make this Guide an interagency document in order to further the harmonization of the procurement of HIV/AIDS products. For the World Bank it takes effect immediately, and an intensive training program will be rolled out for task teams and relevant staff of borrowers and grant recipients.

HIV/AIDS is not just a critical health problem—it is a defining development problem of our time. This Guide materially updates, amplifies, and enhances the Bank's capability, and that of its member countries, to address one of the weakest links in the current fight against the pandemic: appropriate and effective treatment. We trust that it will make a material contribution.

Jean-Louis Sarbib
*Senior Vice President,*
*Human Development Network*

James W. Adams
*Vice President,*
*Operational Policy & Country Services*

# Executive Summary

Antiretroviral therapy (ART) has radically changed the outlook for people who can pay for it or use it in well-resourced health care systems. Living longer, healthier lives, they can become productive and able to care for themselves. ART is not a cure, but it diminishes the viral load and thus reduces damage to the immune system. It also reduces the statistical risk of passing on the virus through whatever route—blood, breast milk, and sexual or other bodily fluids.

Despite some dramatic reductions in the last three years, the costs associated with antiretroviral drugs (ARVs) and other medicines for HIV-related problems are still very high and may remain so. Skilled negotiation and lobbying on behalf of—and by—people with HIV has already had some effect in reducing prices. But even when full advantage is taken of the lowest possible prices on the global market, the annual total cost of ART is still more than the national budget for health care in some countries.

Much higher costs will be incurred in countries that cannot get low-cost supplies for patent or other market reasons. Costs will also be higher if drug resistance develops and more expensive alternative medicines have to be used. So for many countries, assistance from the World Bank, the Global Fund to Fight AIDS, Tuberculosis and Malaria, and other key donors will be essential to make the public health promises of ART a reality, at least for the foreseeable future.

Planners and decision makers must have a clear understanding of the importance of treatment in tackling HIV and ensure that specific services and facilities required for treatment be included in the scaling up effort:

- HIV counseling, testing, and follow-up services for adherence to treatment and psychosocial support.
- Capacity for appropriate management of HIV and opportunistic infections.
- Laboratory services for monitoring treatment.
- Continuous supply of ARVs, other medicines for HIV-related illness, and supplies for laboratory tests and preventive precautions.
- Reliable regulatory mechanisms that ensure the quality of treatment while protecting the individual's right to treatment.

Procurement is only one link in this large network of factors affecting the HIV epidemic. Yet it is clearly vital. Successful treatment depends on continuous, reliable supplies of the necessary medicines and related commodities. Without sustained access to ARVs, the challenge of treatment cannot be met—and the ravages of the epidemic will continue.

## Estimating resource requirements

Estimating the financial and resource requirements of an ART program is a key step in assessing its feasibility and sustainability. Resources for direct treatment are not the only obstacle to introducing and scaling up ART. The lack of physical and human health infrastructure and the inadequacy of systems to distribute essential medicines affect the availability of drugs and financial feasibility. In all cases, the finances for such a program would have to include expenditure on both capacity building (if it is not adequate) and the purchase of drugs and related medical supplies and services—but in varying proportions, depending on skill sets, income levels, epidemic proportions, and local needs in each situation.

## Dealing with patents

Many HIV/AIDS medicines and laboratory products are relatively new and are still protected by patents granted to the originators, usually within countries where the originator has, or expects to have, a significant market. But the patent situation varies widely across countries, affected by such international agreements as the Agreement on Trade-Related

Aspects of Intellectual Property Rights (TRIPS)—so it is important that staff responsible for project implementation assimilate the information in this Guide. Early clarification of the intellectual property rights situation (and of registration requirements and import regulations) will prevent frustration, wasted time and money, and possible litigation.

As a consequence of the Doha Declaration on the TRIPS Agreement and Public Health, adopted by members of the World Trade Organization in November 2001, least developed countries are authorized to forgo the enforcement of patents on pharmaceutical products at least until January 1, 2016. When a least developed country's government and its procurement authority take advantage of this maximum flexibility, HIV/AIDS medicines may be imported (or locally produced) without concern about whether patents on those medicines have been granted within the country.

In addition, several least developed and developing countries are eligible to receive patented ARVs under access programs that have been set up by originator companies, at prices that sometimes may be lower than those of the generic versions.

Developing countries that are not considered "least developed," have the option to override existing patents by issuing a compulsory licensing or government use authorization. A patent is a government grant that permits its holder to exclude third parties from the market for a product, such as an HIV/AIDS–related medicine. A "compulsory license" is an authorization by the government to itself or to a third party to use the patent without the permission of the patent holder. When the government is authorizing its own use, this is also called a "government use" authorization or license, which is a form of compulsory license.

Important HIV/AIDS medicines or supplies are covered by one or more patents in many countries. If the procurement authority wishes to procure a bioequivalent medicine (a generic version) from a party other than the patent holder or its authorized distributor, including by importing the medicine, it may need to authorize procurement under a compulsory license. The TRIPS Agreement, in Article 31, authorizes every government to grant compulsory licenses.

## Managing the supply cycle for better outcomes

The medicines supply cycle comprises all elements required for the establishment and continuity of supplies for health delivery, including medicines and related commodities. It includes four key stages, with a central requirement for good management support, an understanding of the policy and legal frameworks for the supply cycle, and an appreciation that medicines are special commodities that have constraints concerning quality assurance, storage, and use.

Two key elements of the cycle are selection and procurement. But to get good results, it is clear that these must not happen in isolation. All elements of the cycle must function well, and the broader context must be understood so that a holistic and realistic approach can be taken to achieve the best possible results in each setting.

In many countries, a national drug policy will set out approaches to achieving these priorities within the national context. Such policy is also likely to include setting requirements for registration of drugs and limiting who may prescribe, dispense, or sell them. National HIV/AIDS treatment policies must also be consulted, since these set out guidelines for approving HIV treatment regimens and deciding who is entitled to prescribe them.

Some key policy or legal issues that affect procurement include:

- Intellectual property (patent) legislation of medicines—the national patent situation will directly affect what products can be procured from which suppliers and the scope for negotiation of prices.
- Health rights and access to HIV-related treatment when limited supplies, particularly of ARVs, are available, eligibility criteria will be applied to the selection of which members of the population qualify for treatment. This process will affect product selection and quantification and may change as scaling up proceeds.
- Security issues—ARVs for HIV treatment are high in value and thus vulnerable to theft and diversion to illegal markets, or to individuals who are not priority recipients of HIV treatment programs. Planning the supply cycle will have to incorporate effective security measures and a legal framework that allows for sanctions against theft or diversion.

## Deciding who does what

An assessment should be made at an early stage to find out who is already carrying out the tasks related to the supply cycle and to test whether the Bank needs to fund the setting up of new systems and personnel, the use of existing systems, or a combination of both. A preliminary mapping exercise could be used to identify different systems and personnel relevant to the HIV procurements. The strengths and weaknesses of each one should be examined, estimating their willingness and capacity. Bear in mind that a period of rapid growth will be a feature of most HIV treatment programs during scaling up. This rapid growth may strain the capacities and funding of all those who have a part in treatment delivery. It may thus have unforeseen effects on their ability to provide cooperation as programs develop.

When it is clear who can do what for Bank-funded HIV procurement in a specific country, a further assessment of the proposed procurement systems should be carried out. An assessment of the initial situation should also lead to the setting up of monitoring and evaluation criteria and tools for the ongoing performance monitoring of procurement. Performance indicators and monitoring procedures, responsibilities, and financing will be expected.

## Selecting drugs for HIV-related treatment

Public health criteria for selecting ARVs and drugs for opportunistic infections focus on drugs of the greatest importance to satisfy the health needs of the majority of the population of HIV-positive people:

- The selection of drugs should be carried out by a multidisciplinary group, including representatives of the national AIDS committee or council and the national drug formulary committee, together with an HIV specialist doctor, an HIV specialist nurse, a pharmacist with knowledge of available HIV-related medicines, and a procurement specialist. Additional members may be co-opted on an ad hoc basis.
- Drugs should be identified in any printed material by their generic name or international nonproprietary name. But abbreviated chemical names and brand names will also be used when appropriate.
- Drug selection should be based on predetermined criteria, as recommended by the WHO or any existing guidelines of the national drug or AIDS programs.

## Deciding on quantities

It is important to realize that in situations where the HIV/AIDS epidemic or responses to it are expanding, careful judgment will be necessary to arrive at the correct quantities of each commodity needed for procurement and to decide how much to buy. Underestimates will deprive people of necessary treatments or tests. Overestimates may waste resources if limited-shelf-life products expire unused, especially as treatment protocols and diagnostic preferences change.

Three methods can be used for quantification:

- The usage (consumption) method that relies on past use (consumption) records to estimate future need.
- The adjusted usage (adjusted consumption) method that uses data from other facilities, regions, or countries, adjusted or extrapolated to the specific situation on the basis of population coverage or service level.
- The patient morbidity–standard treatment method that estimates the need for specific drugs, based on the expected number of attendances, the prevalence or incidence of diseases, and standard treatment guidelines for the health problems that are to be treated.

## Assessing capacity

In many countries the implementing agencies might lack the capacity to forecast, procure, store, and distribute ARVs and other related medical supplies of the HIV/AIDS care package. It is therefore essential to examine the procurement capacity of the central medical stores for this category of specialized drugs and supplies before deciding on the project's procurement strategy and plan.

If the central medical store is totally deficient and poorly managed, a third alternative must be sought (such as employing a specialized procurement agency or UN agency). This agency can be required, as part of its contractual obligations, to include a training, capacity-building, and technology transfer component intended to strengthen the capacity of the central medical store.

## Using commodities that support the HIV/AIDS program

The HIV/AIDS commodities package is more complex than other products and supplies managed in the public sector:

- A functioning lab infrastructure is essential to support service delivery (equipment, supplies, and human resources).
- The supply chain must be agile and responsive in changing situations, delivering products before they expire or are diverted.
- Service delivery and provider, client, and community education are in the early stages of development, unlike more established health programs.
- A set of comprehensive, interdependent services needs to be provided.
- Decentralizing interventions to the community adds to the complexity of planning, coordination, distribution, and management, because the technical skills for managing these products may be lacking or insufficient.

The HIV/AIDS care package comprises three main product categories: multisource or generic products, limited-source products, and single-source products. Each category corresponds to a distinct procurement strategy:

- Multisource products are pharmaceutically equivalent products that may or may not be therapeutically equivalent, available from different manufacturers. They are well established, normally off patent, and not restricted by continuing intellectual property agreements or other exclusive market arrangements. They are generally available from a wide range of producers, have published pharmacopoeial quality standards, and have available reference standards for quality-control testing.
- Limited-source products are pharmaceutically equivalent products available from a limited number of manufacturers. Newer, they are products usually protected by patents or market-exclusivity arrangements in some countries. Pharmacopoeial quality standards and publicly available reference standards for quality control testing may not yet be available.
- Single-source products are generally under patent with no licensing agreements that allow other firms to manufacture the drugs. Single-source availability may be due to patents, marketing exclusivity, technical challenges of production, or a lack of economic incentives for production by other manufacturers. Pharmacopoeial quality standards

and reference standards for quality control testing might not be publicly available.

## Choosing procurement methods

The market situation of each product, the nature of the medicines and medical supplies, and the critical dates for delivery—are all major factors determining the choice of procurement method. Choices are restricted by the characteristics of medicines and supplies of the HIV/AIDS care package. As already noted, the majority of antiretrovirals and some other HIV-related drugs are either single-source or limited-source products. Other drugs and commodities for opportunistic infections or for basic or palliative care may be multisource but effectively restricted to limited sources in many settings. So, international (or national) competitive bidding without prequalification typically cannot be the preferred method of procurement. Instead, limited international bidding, direct contracting, or shopping may be the most appropriate. The key is to understand what situations are suitable for each of them.

## Pricing

The price of medications can be a significant barrier to HIV/AIDS treatment, especially for ART, a chronic treatment that requires the daily intake of a combination of pharmaceutical compounds. The coverage of health insurance in developing countries is often limited. And when drugs are purchased out-of-pocket, the price of ARVs can make a vital difference for poor people's ability to afford treatment. Even the lowest available prices are unaffordable for most patients in the developing world, where about 3 billion people live on less than US$2 a day. Many HIV-infected patients rely on the subsidized or free provision of antiretroviral treatment by the public sector. For resource-constrained governments in poor countries, the purchase price for the pharmaceutical compounds directly affects the number of patients that can be treated. And lower prices leave more room for investments in the complementary health infrastructure needed to make ART effective.

## Assessing the economic impact of antiretroviral therapy

A primary challenge facing policymakers is estimating the benefits of ART. In the short term, simple models of resource estimation can be used to determine the immediate budgetary implications of ART. Given the resources required for administering ART, it is essential to ensure effectiveness and safety.

Treatments must be proven to work not only in "ideal" clinical trials, with closely monitored patients in a hospital setting, but also in a context that is likely if the program is scaled up. A realistic study should consider compliance and adherence to treatment under alternative strategies, such as directly observed therapy (DOT) strategies, to account for the potential misuse of drugs.

Economic constraints—the fact that other health considerations need to be addressed—call for a critical appraisal of the pros and cons of all technically feasible interventions, and put a premium on rational resource allocation so that health needs can be addressed holistically.

# *Preface*

This Guide sets out principles and advice for the procurement of HIV/AIDS medicines and related supplies for programs scaling up antiretroviral therapy (ART) and associated health services, such as basic and palliative care, disease prevention, treatment of opportunistic infections, and laboratory tests. ART includes the treatment of infected adults and children and the prevention of mother-to-child transmission. A wide range of other commodities—particularly condoms and support for basic living and care—are also essential to support the treatment and prevention of HIV.

The primary audience for this guide is World Bank staff and those responsible for procuring HIV/AIDS medicines and related supplies in Bank-funded programs and projects—which could include either procurement agency staff or technical agency staff. Policymakers and Bank partners will also benefit from the information and advice in the guide.

## The added value of this Guide

Although there already are guidance documents covering the procurement of health goods, this guide specializes in procurement for HIV-related programs for these reasons:

- It focuses on resource-poor settings with little experience of treatment programs that include antiretrovirals (ARVs).

- It discusses newer and more expensive drugs and tests required for ART, which because of cost or scale have not yet become part of essential medicines policy in many countries.
- It draws attention to some of the unpredictable factors associated with the scaling up of ART such as rapid growth in demand, the appearance of new medicines and tests, and sudden changes in markets.
- It provides practical advice on intellectual property rights, a complex but important subject, and it lays out in simple terms the array of options available to national governments.
- It provides references to valuable materials and offers links to readily available instructions and documentation.

## Key resources used in the development of this Guide

The authors of this guide gratefully acknowledge the assistance and cooperation of a number of organizations experienced in responding to the HIV epidemic and in managing and procuring medicines and other health goods. Many of their resources are available on their Web sites, and readers of the guide are recommended to those sites for further information. We particularly acknowledge the following organizations and groups:

- World Health Organization departments:
  - Essential Medicines (WHO/EDM) www.who.int/medicines/ default.shtml
  - HIV/AIDS (WHO/HIV) www.who.int/hiv/en/
  - Regional Office for Africa (AFRO) www.afro.who.int/
  - Blood Safety and Clinical Technology
- The International Dispensary Association (IDA) www.ida.nl/engels/ida.html
- Organization of Eastern Caribbean States (OECS) Pharmaceutical Procurement Service at www.oecs.org/units_pps.htm
- Management Sciences for Health www.msh.org/projects/ rpmplus/1.0.htm
- Médicins Sans Frontières www.accessmed-msf.org
- UNICEF www.unicef.org
- UNFPA www.unfpa.org
- John Snow Incorporated www.jsi.com

# Acknowledgments

This Guide was prepared by a team led by Yolanda Tayler ( World Bank) and comprising Frederick Abbott (Professor of Law, Florida State University), Carmen Perez Casas (Pharmaceutical Policy Consultant), Carsten Fink (World Bank), Carolyn Green (Pharmaceutical Consultant), Achal Prabhala (World Bank), and Juan Rovira (World Bank), with additional contributions by Rudolf Van Puymbroeck and Joan MacNeil (World Bank). Bruce Ross-Larson assisted the team as the principal editor. The work was carried out under the general direction of Armando Araujo and Debrework Zewdie (World Bank).

The following individuals provided helpful comments and suggestions: Clive Bell, Hans Binswanger, Jonathan Brown, Mam Chand, Phil Hay, Alison Micheli, Ok Pannenborg, Sangeeta Raja, Natarajan Raman, Miriam Schneidman, Susan Stout, Josef Wolfbeisser (World Bank), Andreas Seiter (World Bank / IFPMA); Guy-Michel Gershy-Damet, Vincent Habiyambere, Lembit Rago, Andre van Zyl (World Health Organization), Adrian Otten, Jayashree Watal (World Trade Organization), Wilbert Bannenberg (Pharmaceutical Policy Consultant), Henk den Besten, Joseph Spiteri Gonzi, Pascal Verhoeven (International Dispensary Association)and Francis Burnett (Eastern Caribbean Drug Services).

# *Abbreviations*

| | |
|---|---|
| **ART** | Antiretroviral therapy |
| **ARVs** | Antiretrovirals |
| **CDC** | Centers for Disease Control and Prevention |
| **DOTS** | Directly Observed Therapy Short-course program |
| **EU** | European Union |
| **HAART** | highly active antiretroviral therapy |
| **IDA** | International Dispensary Association |
| **IFPMA** | International Federation of Pharmaceutical Manufacturers Associations |
| **MAP** | Multi-country HIV/AIDS Program |
| **OECD** | Organisation for Economic Co-operation and Development |
| **PLWHA** | People living with HIV/AIDS |
| **PMTCT** | Prevention of mother-to-child transmission |
| **TRIPS** | Trade-Related Aspects of Intellectual Property Rights |
| **UNAIDS** | Joint United Nations Programme on HIV/AIDS |
| **UNDP** | United Nations Development Programme |
| **UNICEF** | United Nations Children's Fund |
| **WHO** | World Health Organization |
| **WTO** | World Trade Organization |

All dollars are U.S. dollars unless otherwise stated.

# 1

## *Challenges in Scaling Up Treatment*

The HIV epidemic is an unprecedented challenge to global public health. The prevalence and incidence of HIV are still rising rapidly in many places. And although a few countries have achieved a measure of success in controlling incidence, the number of people needing treatment continues to rise.[1] Even so, antiretroviral therapy (ART) has radically changed the outlook for those who can pay for it or use well-resourced health care systems. By living longer, healthier lives, they can become productive and able to care for themselves.

ART is not a cure, but it diminishes the viral load and thus reduces damage to the immune system. It also reduces the statistical risk of passing on the virus through whatever route—sexual or other bodily fluids, blood, and breast milk. Treatment to prevent mother-to-child HIV transmission during birth or through breastfeeding can reduce pediatric infection rates by as much as 70 percent when combined with care for the mother and changes in feeding practices. So treatment is also a preventive measure, reducing the chances of transmission by infected persons and enabling people with HIV to resist opportunistic infections, considerably reducing illnesses.

Most people with HIV are in poorer countries or in marginal groups and do not have access to ART. Some 40 million people live with HIV in

---

[1] For more detail, see www.unaids.org/Unaids/EN/Resources/epidemiology.asp.

developing countries—about 6 million in need of treatment. But by 2003 only 400,000 people actually had access to treatment, representing a treatment coverage of 7 percent. Until recently, it was feared that poor infrastructure and lack of resources would prevent ART from being successful in these situations. Not so. Pilot studies have pointed to good adherence levels and sustained treatment. The cost of antiretroviral drugs (ARVs) has also dropped and will likely drop further for use in these situations.

The United Nations General Assembly Special Session on HIV/AIDS in 2001 emphasized the complementarity of HIV care and prevention, urging governments to provide the highest attainable standards of care, including ART. Many governments, and the world of business, are now looking for ways to respond. The World Bank and other institutions have made support for ART an important element of their support for improving public health and containing the HIV epidemic.

But scaling up of treatment with ARVs and other HIV-related medicines presents serious practical challenges. Countries and communities naturally have many other competing priorities. Scarce resources and limited capacity mean that many countries face problems in reaching existing goals for health services and social support. Lack of infrastructure is not a reason to delay ART, but scaling up must include measures to improve the general context of health care and support. And plans for scaling up ART have to be developed within the local context to be acceptable and effective. Those in authority and people from communities can together provide powerful support for treatment programs and be instrumental in their success.

Planners and decisionmakers must have a clear understanding of the importance of treatment in tackling HIV and ensure that specific services and facilities required for treatment be included in the scaling-up effort:

- HIV counseling, testing, and follow-up services for adherence to treatment and psychosocial support.
- Capacity for appropriate management of HIV and opportunistic infections.
- Laboratory services for monitoring treatment.
- Continuous supply of ARVs, other medicines for HIV-related illness, and supplies for laboratory tests and preventive precautions.
- Reliable regulatory mechanisms that ensure the quality of treatment while protecting the individual's right to treatment.

Access to ART by a large cross-section of the population will be partly constrained by the rate at which health services develop. But there is likely to be pressure for treatment, with more people seeking HIV testing to be eligible for it. Official estimates of HIV prevalence are thought to be only the tip of the iceberg in many countries—"real" levels are estimated to be up to 10 times the official figures in some countries. Other related services must also be scaled up: counseling, HIV testing, laboratory monitoring, information and education for patients, health care support, local community support, and general awareness campaigns.

Despite some dramatic reductions in the past three years, the costs associated with ARVs and other medicines for HIV-related problems are still very high and may remain so in the future. Skilled negotiation and lobbying on behalf of—and by—people with HIV has already had some effect in reducing prices. But even when full advantage is taken of the lowest possible prices on the global market, the annual cost of ART is more than the national budget for health care in some countries. Much higher costs will be incurred in countries that cannot get low-cost supplies for patent or other market reasons. Costs will also be higher if drug resistance develops and more expensive alternative medicines have to be used. So far in many countries, assistance from the the World Bank, the Global Fund to Fight AIDS, Tuberculosis and Malaria and other key donors is essential to make the public health promises of ART a reality, at least in the foreseeable future.

But the sustainability of an ART program is only partly a question of external funding. The contributions of different sectors of society will be vital, providing active acceptance and use of ART and involvement in service provision and sharing of information, understanding, and lessons. In rapidly changing situations, measures for sustainability are impossible to quantify, but the outcomes of successful treatment programs must at least do the following:

- Reduce HIV–related morbidity and mortality—to reduce the burden of disease on the community.
- Improve the quality of life for people with HIV and their families— to reduce the burden of care and increase the ability to be productive.
- Reduce levels of the virus in the community—to reduce the incidence of new or reinfected cases.
- Restore family and social structures fractured by high rates of death and illness.

Procurement is only one link in this large network of factors affecting the HIV epidemic. Yet, it is clearly vital. Successful treatment depends on continuous, reliable supplies of the necessary medicines and related commodities. Without sustained access to antiretrovirals, the challenge of treatment cannot be met—and the ravages of the epidemic will continue.

## The economic impact of HIV/AIDS and ART

A primary challenge facing policymakers is estimating the benefits of ART. In the short term, simple models of resource estimation can be used to determine the immediate budgetary implications of ART. Given the resources required for administering ART, it is essential to ensure effectiveness and safety. One way to do this is to start by reviewing the evidence on the efficacy and safety of ART in settings comparable to those of the country where ART is to be scaled up. Effects of malnutrition and other illnesses should also be assessed. If no clear evidence is available, an appropriate experimental study should be considered, involving clinical trials with a control group.

Treatments must be proven to work not only in "ideal" clinical trials, with closely monitored patients in a hospital setting, but also in a context that is likely if the program is scaled up. A realistic study should consider compliance (regularity in taking treatment) and adherence (long-term continuity) to treatment under alternative strategies, such as directly observed therapy (DOT) to account for the potential misuse of drugs.

Because experimental data are expensive and difficult to obtain, a simulation model could be developed in the short term to estimate the economic, demographic, and health impacts of alternative HIV/AIDS strategies. Such a model would consistently project the evolution of the epidemic and its effects using the best information available. It could also become a learning tool for assessing the medium-term and long-term effects of interventions and strategies. The objective would not be to pretend that accurate forecasts are possible, but to get a sense of the magnitude of the effects of interventions for planning and policy design, in relation to a baseline. Such a model could also help in cost-effectiveness and cost-benefit analyses of HIV/AIDS–related interventions.

Economic constraints—the fact that other health considerations need to be addressed—call for a critical appraisal of the pros and cons of all technically feasible interventions and put a premium on rational resource allocation so that health needs can be addressed holistically.

To satisfy the political demand and social expectations for ART, pilot projects could pave the way for a future scaling up. Such pilots might have a strong research and evaluation component to increase knowledge on the feasibility and performance of ART options in limited-resource settings, such as rural areas. The pilots should provide evidence on such issues as compliance and adherence to treatments and the effectiveness of care that prevents a diversion of medication to unintended people or black markets.

Whatever the scale of ART considered, the purchase of quality drugs at the lowest feasible prices is a key issue. There is significant price variation worldwide for the same medicine or therapeutic class. Prices may vary by as much as 300 percent in the developing world alone. Accordingly, cost savings may be substantial depending on the drug purchased.

## Estimating resource requirements

Estimating the financial and resource requirements of an ART program is a key step in assessing its feasibility and sustainability. Resources for direct treatment are not the only obstacle to introducing and scaling up an ART program. The lack of physical and human health infrastructure and the inadequacy of systems to distribute essential medicines affect the availability of drugs and financial feasibility. In all cases, the finances for such a program would have to include expenditure on both capacity building (if it is not adequate) and the purchase of drugs and related medical supplies and services—but in varying proportions, depending on skill sets, income levels, epidemic proportions, and local needs.

Some key questions follow:

- Who should receive care?
- Which are the treatments to be provided?
- What is the adequate time horizon of the estimation?
- What is the degree of accuracy required?

Planning and estimating the cost of a comprehensive ART program, should start with the gathering of baseline data concerning demographic trends, epidemiological and medical information and any existing cost data. In addition, data on number of patients to be treated, protocols for the allocation of facility space and staff time, treatment protocols for opportunistic infections, second line treatment regimens for drug resistant patients, and the prevention of mother-to-child transmission should also be entered into the model. With these inputs, a proper costing model can produce estimates for total costs and resource requirements under the various policy scenarios for an ART program.[2]

The World Bank consultation in Burkina Faso illustrates such an exercise (see Annex A). The uses and implications of such costing estimates must be carefully considered. A projected increase in health care costs or an additional burden on the state exchequer (even with low-priced medicines) might be better interpreted as an urgent signal for additional donor funds than a situation where meaningful intervention is beyond reach.

## Long-term economic effect of HIV/AIDS and other considerations

One important economic impact of HIV/AIDS is the potentially disastrous decline in human capital. A team of scholars estimated the long-run economic costs of AIDS in South Africa:[3]

- Existing estimates of the macroeconomic costs of AIDS, as measured by a reduction in the growth rate of GDP, are modest (between 0.3 percent and 1.5 percent annually). They are underestimates.
- HIV/AIDS does more than destroy existing human capital. Because it affects mainly young adults, it weakens the mechanism for one generation to transmit knowledge and abilities to the next. Cumulatively, this weakening across multiple generations can be devastating.

---

[2] Partners for the Health Reformplus (PHRplus) project, the U.S. Agency for International Development's flagship project in health policy and systems strengthening, has developed the AIDS-TREATCOST (ATC) antiretroviral modeling software to determine costs of implementing ARV programs. For further information readers should consult www.phrplus.org/hiv-atc.html.

[3] Clive Bell, Shantayanan Devarajan, and Hans Gersbach. 2003. *The Long-run Economic Costs of AIDS: Theory and Application to South Africa.* World Bank, Washington D.C. Available at www1.worldbank.org/hiv_aids/docs/BeDeGe_BP_total2.pdf.

- With high premature adult mortality, there may be a progressive collapse of human capital and productivity.
- The policy instruments available to a government in this situation are:
  - Spending money to contain the disease and treating those infected
  - Supporting orphans, particularly their education
  - Using taxes to finance these expenses.

Applying this model to South Africa yielded the following results. Without AIDS, the country showed modest economic growth and universal education in three generations. Without *anything* being done to combat the epidemic as it currently exists in South Africa, the study estimated a "complete economic collapse" in three generations.[3]

Importantly, the study also focused on the relative long-term economic benefits of different levels of intervention. With optimal spending on the right programs, it was estimated that growth will continue, though at a slower rate than without AIDS. Without pooling (defined as a social protection system where all children are cared for by extended members of

---

### Box 1.1 The long-term economic consequences of AIDS in South Africa

Clive Bell, Shanta Devarajan, and Hans Gersbach argue that AIDS (in the South African context) has serious long-term economic implications:

- It reduces incentives and the means to invest in children's education.
- It reduces the transmission of knowledge from parent to child.
- It creates a vicious cycle, since children's ability to invest in their children's education is lower, and so on.

So, the long-term economic impacts may well have been massively underestimated in previous studies. The key policy implications from their paper might be summed up as follows:

- Spend more on public goods to reduce premature mortality (an additional 3 percent to 4 percent of GDP).
- Consider lump-sum subsidies to nuclear families.
- Consider school attendance subsidies for young people.

Source: Bell, Devarajan, and Gersbach. 2003. *The Long-run Economic Costs of AIDS: Theory and Application to South Africa.* World Bank, Washington D.C. Available at www1.worldbank.org/hiv_aids/docs/BeDeGe_BP_total2.pdf.

## Box 1.2 ART and drug resistance

ART, particularly in resource-limited settings, must be carefully planned, implemented, and monitored if it is to limit drug resistance. Indeed, suboptimal ARV regimens can lead to drug resistance. Trials and experiences in resource-limited settings show a sustained immunological benefit through ART, despite a partial viral rebound. Persistent clinical benefits can be observed, despite the greater drug resistance. That resistance limits but does not eliminate the usefulness of highly-active antiretroviral therapy (HAART).

Data from the United States and Europe show:

- Drug resistance in about 5 percent to 15 percent of newly infected cases.
- Drug resistance in about 50 percent of treated patients.

Why the difference between contemporary and earlier cases? To some extent, it is the legacy of earlier, suboptimal treatment therapies. With HAART, the risk of drug resistance is lower in contemporary cases. To maximize viral suppression, maximize treatment adherence, and minimize infection, regimens should be as potent and simple as possible.

There is no empirical evidence that nonadherence and viral resistance are a greater problem for patients treated in developing countries. Yet, there is a risk of spreading resistant viruses if treatment regimens are not followed.

What makes ART programs work?

- Using standard regimens, with fixed dose therapies. Making monitoring less complicated, with simplified diagnostics. Supporting adherence to treatment, making good use of all human resources.
- Working with communities.

The challenge is to scale up treatment programs. To ensure success against possible drug resistance, it is crucial to implement programs that address greater community involvement in treatment (beyond traditional health care workers) and that come up with strategies for better adherence on the part of the community.

Source: Daniel Kuritzkes. 2003. "Provision of ARV Therapy in Resource-Limited Settings: The Challenges of Drug Resistance and Adherence." World Bank-sponsored workshop.

the family), growth will be slower. Without school attendance subsidies, future economic growth was estimated as "distinctly sluggish."

Another important consequence of ART is its effect on prevention. Evidence from Haiti suggests that people receiving ART are less likely to reinfect others.[4]

---

[4] Sally Blower and Paul Farmer (2003), "Predicting the Public Health Impact of Antiretrovirals: Preventing HIV in Developing Countries" *AIDScience*, 3(11).

Concurring evidence comes from Jean Paul Moatti,[5] who surveyed the sexual behaviors of HIV-infected patients in Côte d'Ivoire in 2000. The study compared a sizable group of HIV-infected people, some of whom were being treated and others not. Patients treated with ARVs were found to be more likely than those not treated to have one main partner, to have informed at least one member of their family about their HIV serostatus, to have systematically used condoms with their main partner, and to have systematically used condoms with occasional partners.

## References

These are the documents used to draft this chapter.

BURKINAVI. 2002. "Etude clinique prospective et ouverte d'une cohorte de patients infectés par le VIH et traits par tritherapie antiretrovirale au Burkina Faso, dans le contexte d'une observance renforcée." National AIDS Research Agency, Paris.

Burkina Faso, Management Committee. 2002. "Requetê du Burkina Faso au Fonds Global, Lutte contre le Sida, la Tuberculose et le Paludisme." Ouagadougou.

ESTHER. 2001–02. *Initiative Ensemble pour une Solidarite Therapeutique Hospitalière en Réseau. France-Senegal. Document de Project* « 2002–2004 ». France/Senegal National Council for the Fight against AIDS, Senegal.

UNDP (United Nations Development Programme). 2001. "Rapport sur le developpement humain. Burkina Faso, 2001: La lutte contre le SIDA. Geneva.

Traore, A., A. Keita, and J. B. Zoungrana. 2002. "Revue des Dépenses Publiques. Secteur de la Santé 1996–1999." Ministry of Economy and Finance, Burkina Faso.

Schneidman, Miriam. 2002. "The Health System and the Poor: Draft report on Burkina Faso." World Bank, Washington, D.C.

---

[5] Jean Paul Moatti, and others. 2003. *Economics of AIDS and Access to HIV/AIDS Care in Developing Countries.* Agence nationale de recherches sur le sida (ANRS), Paris.

# 2

## *Intellectual Property Rights: A Concise Guide*

### Introduction to this concise guide

The procurement of HIV/AIDS–related medicines and supplies is directly affected by rights in intellectual property, most notably patents. The subject of intellectual property is very complex. Some areas are confusing even to the most highly trained specialists. Yet procurement authorities cannot avoid the subject. When supplies of low-cost, high-quality medicines are sought from so-called "generic" producers, holders of patents on those same medicines may object. But procurement authorities may be able to overcome patent obstacles by using "flexibilities" established by international agreement. These flexibilities were recently affirmed by the World Trade Organization as it addressed the relationship between intellectual property rights and public health. Annex B contains a detailed discussion of how patents and other intellectual property rights affect medicines procurement. This chapter outlines the basics a procurement authority should know, but, of necessity, presents only a simplified treatment of the subject. Annex B should be consulted for a more complete discussion.

## How patents affect medicines procurement

When a new medicine is developed, its inventor (or originator) may be granted a patent. The patent gives the originator the right to prevent others from making and selling that medicine, creating a monopoly. The period of patent protection is now commonly 20 years.

When a procurement authority attempts to purchase medicines, such as ARVs, it may find that there are supplies available on the world market from generic producers, as well as from the originator. How can that be? In some countries, patent protection for the medicine may not have been sought, or it may have expired, allowing generic producers to enter the market. Some countries only recently began offering product patent protection for medicines, and some countries even today do not provide such protection (for example, India until January 1, 2005). Generics may be produced and sold lawfully in these countries, even if there is patent protection elsewhere. The procurement authority should investigate whether there are generic medicines available, either in-country or from a foreign supplier, at prices below those available from originators.

If generic medicines are available in-country (because the originator's product was not patented there, or because the patent has expired, or because one or more licenses have been granted, or because patents do not need to be enforced in the country in accordance with WTO rules), then patents will not pose a problem for limited-source or multi-source procurement.

If generic medicines are available from foreign suppliers, this does not necessarily mean that they can be lawfully imported because the originator may hold a patent "in-country" and may try to use it to block importation. This, however, is only the beginning of the story.

## Least developed countries

In November 2001, an important decision in favor of least developed countries was made by the World Trade Organization (WTO), which oversees the way patents are used in trade. It was decided that at least until January 1, 2016, least developed countries could elect *not to "enforce" patents or data protection rules* that might affect the procurement of medicines. In least developed countries, originator companies may not have applied for, or they may choose not to enforce, patents for ARVs and other HIV/AIDS–related medicines and supplies. Nevertheless, in situations in which patents are present and in which they might interfere with the procurement of generic medicines, the government can make a decision not to enforce patents or data protection rules. Such a decision would comply with the rules set up by the WTO.

In circumstances where the government decides not to enforce patents or data protection rules, it should adopt a decision to this effect since generic suppliers may be reluctant to make products available if there is risk that they will be subject to liability (see figure 2.1).

As an alternative to the special right granted by the WTO not to enforce patents and data protection rules, least developed countries may also use the flexibilities available to developing countries, which are discussed in the next section. However, it is very important for procurement authorities in least developed countries to be aware of their special rights and opportunities.

## Developing countries

Procurement authorities in developing countries may investigate whether they are covered by existing access programs and can purchase originator drugs at prices at or below the generic level. As discussed below, they have the option to issue a "compulsory license." Originator companies being aware of this option on the side of the government may offer either lower prices for their products or a voluntary license for import or manufacture of generics.

If a government does not want to negotiate or cannot reach an agreement with the originator on price or voluntary license, it can obtain generic medicines by issuing a "government use" license, which is a form of "compulsory license." A government use license authorizes the procurement authority to make (or purchase) and distribute a medicine without the consent or approval of the patent holder (see figure 2.2). The patent law of virtually every country allows the government to use private patents, with provision for providing adequate remuneration to the patent holder. If a government is using this option to secure low-cost supplies of medicines to address HIV/AIDS, it will be justified in providing a modest royalty to the patent holder because of the overwhelming public interest in addressing this urgent public health problem. (By way of illustration, when legislation was introduced in Canada to implement compulsory licensing for

**Figure 2.1  Intellectual property rights checklist: least developed country**

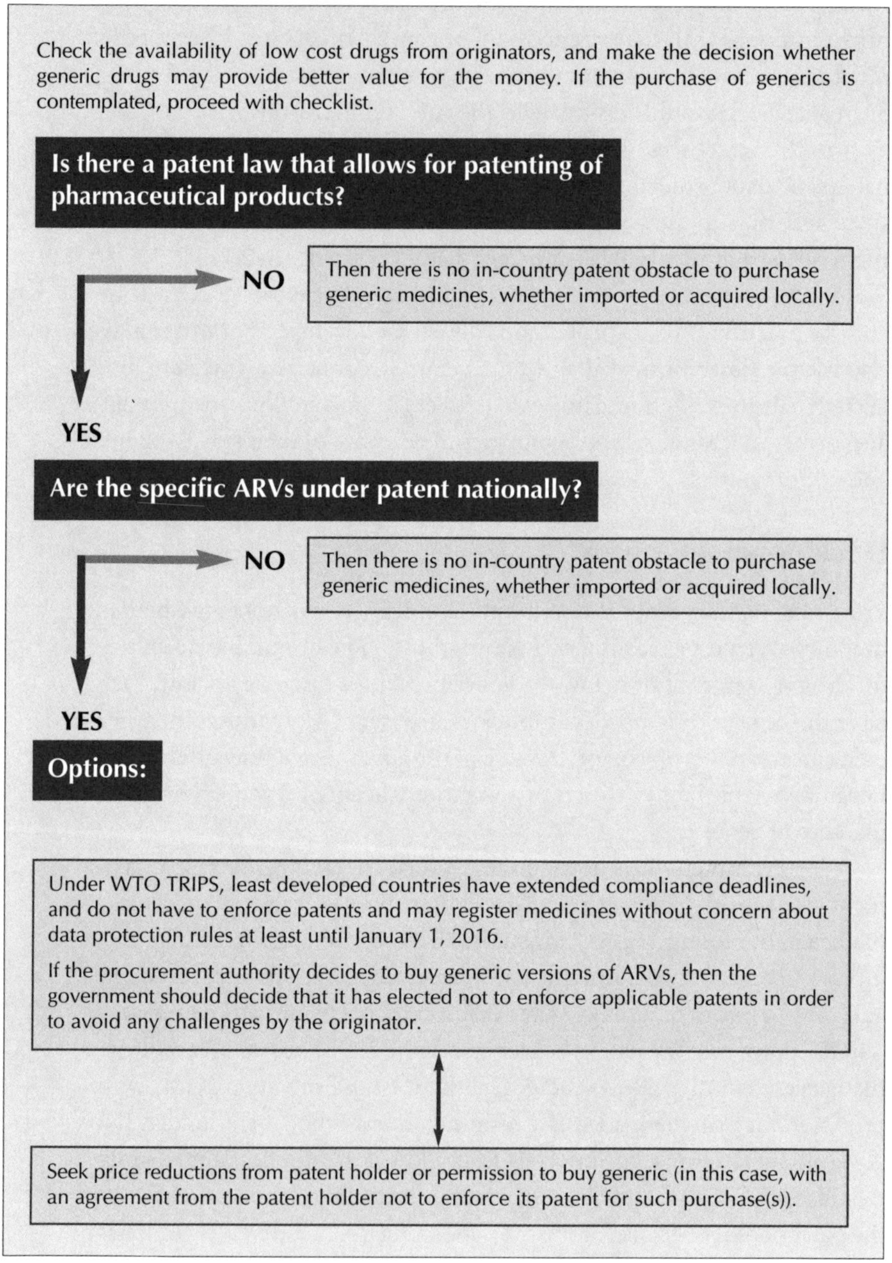

Check the availability of low cost drugs from originators, and make the decision whether generic drugs may provide better value for the money. If the purchase of generics is contemplated, proceed with checklist.

**Is there a patent law that allows for patenting of pharmaceutical products?**

**NO** — Then there is no in-country patent obstacle to purchase generic medicines, whether imported or acquired locally.

**YES**

**Are the specific ARVs under patent nationally?**

**NO** — Then there is no in-country patent obstacle to purchase generic medicines, whether imported or acquired locally.

**YES**

**Options:**

Under WTO TRIPS, least developed countries have extended compliance deadlines, and do not have to enforce patents and may register medicines without concern about data protection rules at least until January 1, 2016.

If the procurement authority decides to buy generic versions of ARVs, then the government should decide that it has elected not to enforce applicable patents in order to avoid any challenges by the originator.

Seek price reductions from patent holder or permission to buy generic (in this case, with an agreement from the patent holder not to enforce its patent for such purchase(s)).

export to meet public health needs in developing countries, a royalty of 2 percent of the value of the pharmaceuticals exported was proposed.)

National patent law will usually indicate the steps that should be taken to issue a government use license. WTO rules allow flexibility for the government to act without prior notification to or negotiation with the patent holder. Government use licensing procedures are typically much easier to follow than procedures applied to businesses seeking to obtain "compulsory licenses" for private use. If national patent law does not already include procedures for government use licensing, this does not mean that the government cannot authorize its own use of patents. It should simply follow the rules laid out by the WTO, which recognizes the special nature of "government use" licensing.

There is one wrinkle to add to this discussion. What if the procurement authority wants to employ a government use license, but there is no domestic producer that can manufacture the medicines and there is no existing generic supply available from foreign countries because of applicable patent rules? In this case, the procurement authority may request a foreign country to issue a compulsory license for export. This is a new feature of WTO law adopted on August 30, 2003. WTO rules lay down the steps that should be followed in making and implementing these requests, and the Global HIV/AIDS Program at the World Bank can provide information and guidance on how to use this new flexibility.

## A note on "parallel imports"

All countries, whether developed, developing, or least developed, are permitted by international rules to authorize parallel imports of medicines. What does this mean? It means that a procurement authority can shop for the lowest-priced patented medicine available on the market in any country, purchase that medicine in a foreign country, and import it without the consent of the patent holder in its own country. Why? Because the same patent holder in the foreign country will already have earned money on the lawful first sale of the medicine, and it need not be compensated again when the medicine is imported. There are different ways that countries treat parallel imports (some allow parallel imports, some do not). If a decision is made to take advantage of parallel imports, the patent law of the importing country should authorize this practice. In chapter 6, "What role

**Figure 2.2 Intellectual property rights checklist: developing country**

Check the availability of low cost drugs from originators, and make the decision whether generic drugs may provide better value for the money. If the purchase of generics is contemplated, proceed with checklist.

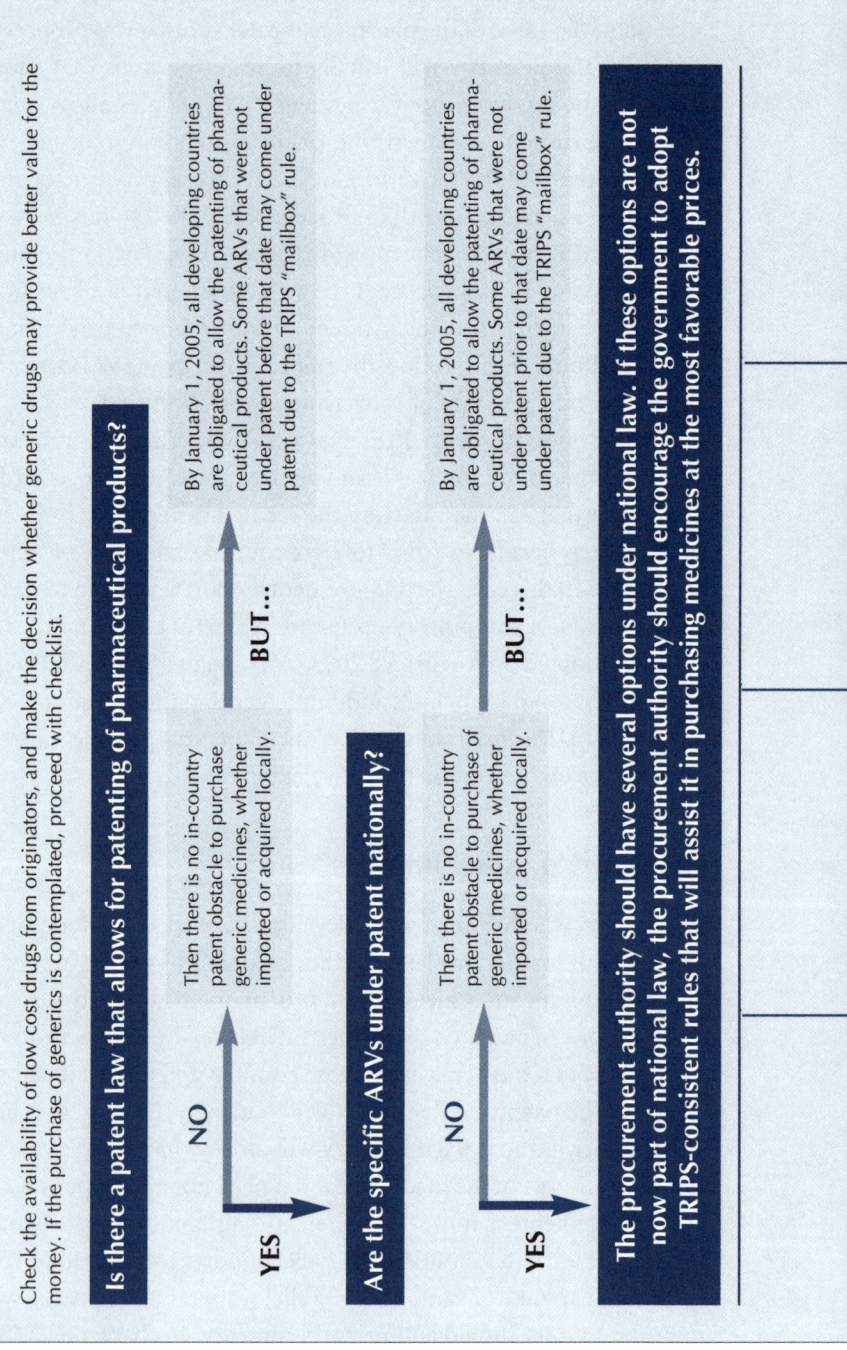

**Is there a patent law that allows for patenting of pharmaceutical products?**

NO → Then there is no in-country patent obstacle to purchase generic medicines, whether imported or acquired locally.

YES →

**BUT...** → By January 1, 2005, all developing countries are obligated to allow the patenting of pharmaceutical products. Some ARVs that were not under patent before that date may come under patent due to the TRIPS "mailbox" rule.

**Are the specific ARVs under patent nationally?**

NO → Then there is no in-country patent obstacle to purchase of generic medicines, whether imported or acquired locally.

YES →

**BUT...** → By January 1, 2005, all developing countries are obligated to allow the patenting of pharmaceutical products. Some ARVs that were not under patent prior to that date may come under patent due to the TRIPS "mailbox" rule.

**The procurement authority should have several options under national law. If these options are not now part of national law, the procurement authority should encourage the government to adopt TRIPS-consistent rules that will assist it in purchasing medicines at the most favorable prices.**

## PARALLEL IMPORTING

The procurement authority may "parallel import" the medicine. This means that it will buy the patented version of the medicine at the lowest price available on the world market, regardless of where the medicine is placed on the market. National law should, however, authorize this under a rule of "international exhaustion" of patent rights. Otherwise, the patent holder within the country may be able to block the importation.

Seek price reduction from patent holder or permission to buy generic (in this case, with an agreement from the patent holder not to enforce its patent for such purchase). The procurement authority is not obligated to pursue these options with the patent holder.

A procurement authority acting on behalf of the government may acquire ARVs from a private party operating under compulsory license. But if the procurement authority is initiating a process to acquire medicines without consent of the patent holder, it would ordinarily act under a "government use" authorization.

## COMPULSORY LICENSING AND GOVERNMENT USE

The procurement authority may invoke national legislation that permits government use of third party patents in cases of national emergency or circumstances of extreme urgency (the HIV/AIDS pandemic qualifies for such treatment), or for public noncommercial use. The government use license can be used by the procurement authority (or a third party acting on its behalf) to import generic ARVs, or it can be used to authorize local manufacturing. The government use license should authorize registration of the generic ARVs, if it is not already registered under a regulatory review exception. The government is not required to negotiate for a voluntary license from the patent holder, but will be required to pay "adequate remuneration in the circumstances of [the] case, taking into account the economic value of the authorization." The government will determine the amount of the remuneration to be paid to the patent holder, and may take into account its own public health budget and the importance of addressing its people's health needs.

A generic pharmaceutical producer may seek a compulsory license from the government to make or import ARVs. If the private party is addressing HIV/AIDS, it may also be able to avoid prior negotiations with the patent holder because it is dealing with a national emergency or other circumstance of extreme urgency. If the ARVs are to be imported and if the exporter produces under a compulsory license but its production is not predominantly for the supply of its domestic market, then the system established under the WTO's August 30, 2003 "paragraph 6" decision must be applied.

**Figure 2.3  Can a country use World Bank funds to procure generic ARVs?**

Country A in Africa, a donor recipient under the Multi-country HIV/AIDS Program (MAP), asks the World Bank whether funds it receives under this program can be used to purchase generically produced ARVs from India.

Country A: Can MAP funds from the World Bank be used to buy generic ARVs produced in India?

World Bank policy is that MAP recipient countries may use those funds to procure ARVs in any circumstances that are legal. So long as the said ARVs are manufactured and distributed in accordance with relevant standards of quality, safety, and efficacy, there is no preference regarding whether such ARVs are purchased from a patent holder with respect to such medicine or from a vendor of the same medicine that produces and sells under circumstances in which the consent of the patent holder is not required.

Question: Are medicines patentable in Country A, and if so what ARVs have been patented there?

Country A's legislation allowed for the patenting of medicines. The law there also included provisions allowing the minister responsible for administration of the patent registry to direct that a patented invention may be exploited by the government without the consent of the patent holder when "in the vital public interest," with adequate remuneration to the patent holder to be fixed by the government. The law defined the "vital public interest" to include matters of public health. A source of patent legislation is the publicly accessible database known as the Collection of Laws for Electronic Access (CLEA) maintained by the World Intellectual Property Organization (WIPO) at www.wipo.int. However, records in this database may not be complete and WIPO may be contacted directly.

To answer the question of which ARVs were specifically under patent in Country A, the offices of Médicins Sans Frontières in Paris were contacted.

**Médicins Sans Frontières has spent several years compiling information on the patent status of ARVs in various developing countries.**

Fortunately, Country A is one of those for which Médicins Sans Frontières has compiled detailed information. The chart furnished by Médicins Sans Frontières indicated that 10 ARVs were under patent in Country A, a number of them on Country A's standard treatment list.

The responsible officials then examined Country A's situation on WTO rules. As a least developed WTO Member, Country A was allowed to disregard patents on pharmaceutical products and any obligations it might have to protect rights in data submitted for regulatory purposes. Country A was not required to follow the procedures established in its patent law for issuing an authorization for government use (or to pay remuneration to patent holders).

**It was thus determined that it was for the government of Country A to decide whether or not to exercise the discretion it has to disregard patents on ARVs and any associated regulatory data rules.**

If Country A exercises this discretion, the import of ARVs from India would raise no concerns under the terms of the TRIPS Agreement.

The government might seek voluntary agreement from relevant patent holders not to enforce patents or data protection.

**Each least developed country must decide for itself (within its constitutional structure) how its internal authority will be allocated and the government medicines procurement authority may have the discretion to disregard patents to procure lower-cost, safe, and effective generic ARVs.**

is there for parallel imported drugs?", it is noted that parallel importing typically does not involve purchasing directly from the patent holder, and that the opportunity for cost saving will vary depending on the nature of the transaction. In any transaction involving medicines it is important to assure adequate supervision of the supply chain. Medicines imported directly from originators under access programs are typically prevented by contract from being re-exported, and such contract terms should be respected.

## Registration and data exclusivity

Before a medicine is placed on the market in a country, it is usually subject to registration and/or marketing approval. Originators may attempt to use patents and data protection rules to block the registration or marketing approval of generic equivalents. This is a complicated subject, particularly when only private companies are involved. For purposes of HIV/AIDS medicines procurement, the discussion can be simplified. First, WTO rules expressly authorize least developed countries to ignore patents and data protection rules until January 1, 2016. Action by least developed countries to take advantage of this flexibility should extend to the registration process. Second, the WTO has already decided that governments at any stage of development may allow generic producers to register medicines without the consent of patent holders, and this flexibility should be used by national authorities. Developing country governments can prevent disputes from arising by expressly including a regulatory review exception in the country's patent legislation or regulation. Also, rules on data protection only address the "unfair commercial use" of certain information. When a government is approving the use of a medicine for HIV/AIDS treatment in its health care system, it is not making unfair commercial use of originator data. It is addressing an urgent public health need.

The Bank encourages procurement authorities to lawfully purchase the lowest-cost medicines that meet accepted standards of quality, safety, and efficacy. This chapter provides basic information procurement authorities need for addressing intellectual property rights questions that arise as they go about this. More detailed treatment of these questions is contained in Annex B.

# 3

## *Managing the Supply Cycle for Better Outcomes*

The medicines supply cycle comprises all elements required for the establishment and continuity of supplies for health delivery, including medicines and related commodities (figure 3.1). It includes four key stages, with a central requirement for good management support, an understanding of the policy and legal frameworks for the supply cycle, and an appreciation that medicines are special commodities that have constraints concerning quality assurance, storage, and use.[6]

Two key elements of the cycle—selection and procurement—will be discussed in detail in this guide. But to get good results, it is clear that these must not happen in isolation. All elements of the cycle must function well, and the broader context must be understood so that a holistic and realistic approach can be taken to achieve the best possible results in each setting.

The key results are appropriate and effective treatment for people with HIV, which will provide public health benefits in containing and mitigating the effects of the HIV epidemic—in other words, providing medicines of the right kind, of the right quality, at a reasonable price, at the right quantities, where they are needed, and at the right times. Programs

---

[6] Key source for this chapter is *Managing Drug Supply*, West Hartford, CT: Kumarian Press. ISBN 1-56549-047-9. With grateful acknowledgement to the authors and to Management Sciences for Health; material has been adapted to include HIV-related policy and procurement issues.

**Figure 3.1 The medicines supply cycle**

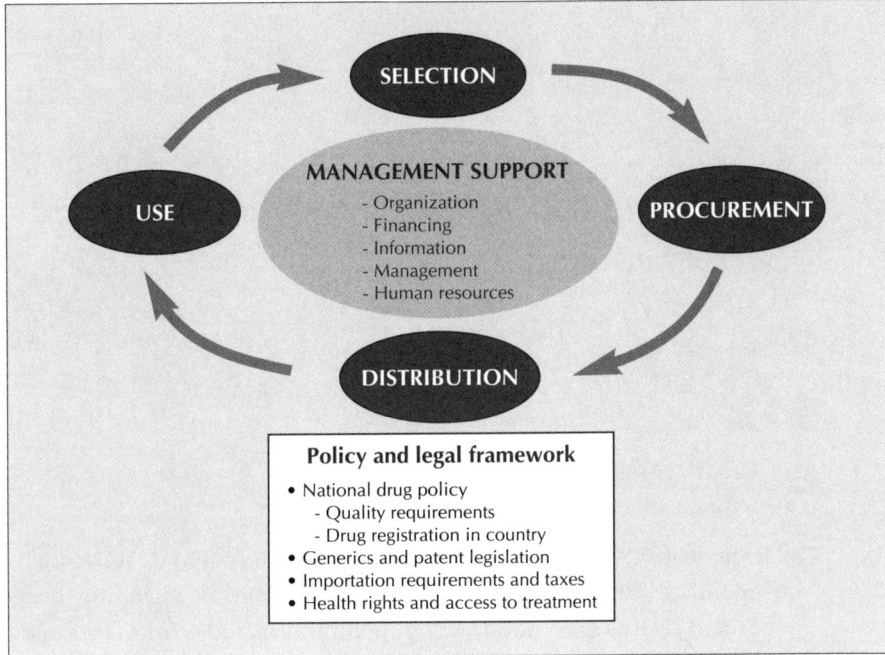

to provide HIV/AIDS-related drugs, including ARVs, will fail if procurement services do not reach this goal.

To achieve the desired results, the following are required:

- Careful choice of medicines according to national or World Health Organization (WHO) guidelines.
- Procurement of value-for-money medicines of proven good quality.
- Effective and efficient distribution systems right up to the point of use, ensuring no gaps in supply.
- Rational prescription and use of medicines to support high adherence levels and prevent wastage, unwanted effects, or drug resistance.

In many countries, a national drug policy will set out approaches to achieving these priorities within the national context. Such policy is also likely to include setting requirements for registration of drugs and limiting who may prescribe, dispense, or sell them. National HIV/AIDS treatment policies must also be consulted, since these set out guidelines for approving HIV treatment regimens and who is entitled to prescribe them.

But some countries do not yet have well-developed drug policies, or HIV medicines may not yet have been included in HIV policies drawn up before HIV treatment became a feasible public health option. The concept of scaling up ART, very new in most countries, has yet to be properly mainstreamed in health policy and HIV care documents. In these situations it will also be necessary to consult global or regional policy statements and treatment guidelines provided by the WHO and the Joint United Nations Programme on HIV/AIDS (UNAIDS) to gain a full picture of what is required and what is feasible in each country.

Other key policy or legal issues that affect procurement include:

- Intellectual property (patent) legislation of medicines—the national patent situation will directly affect what products can be procured from which suppliers and what scope there will be for negotiation on prices.
- Health rights and access to HIV-related treatment—when limited supplies, particularly of ARVs, are available, eligibility criteria will be applied to selection of which members of the population qualify for treatment. This will affect product selection and quantification and may change as scaling up proceeds. For example, some programs will start with prevention of mother-to-child transmission, and progress only later to adult treatments. There will be an implicit rationing mechanism in place in most countries, as the demand for these drugs is likely to exceed the supply. Hence, while recognizing that each country will identify its own eligibility criteria for patient selection the most important factors will be to make this process transparent and participatory, including involving PLWHA.
- Security issues—ARVs for HIV treatment are high value and thus vulnerable to theft and diversion to illegal markets or to individuals who are not priority recipients of HIV treatment programs. So, planning the supply cycle will therefore have to incorporate effective security measures and a legal framework that allows for sanctions against theft or diversion.

## Who does what?

Establishing an effective procurement cycle requires a clear understanding of the tasks and an alignment of capacities and responsibilities.

## What tasks need to be done?

A more detailed outline of the supply cycle illustrates the stages required (figure 3.2). Each stage requires a set of decisions and actions to be taken, but these must also interact with the decisions and actions taken in the preceding and following phases. For instance, reconciling funds available with expressed needs will depend on a meticulous assessment of needs and a clear drug selection policy. It will also depend on what procurement methods and suppliers can be used, because these affect prices and delivery periods.

With changes in the epidemic and the processes of scaling up, HIV treatment situations are likely to be in a state of change. The quantities, prices, and choices of drugs required may therefore also be changing. This makes quantification and procurement less certain than in other situations where public health needs are fairly constant and can be dealt with using routine supplies of essential drugs or small supplies of specialist drugs.

Procurement officers will manage many of the steps illustrated here. But they will have to collaborate closely with technical and policy staff to keep the cycle moving smoothly and successfully. Managing medicines procurement involves three major steps—planning, implementation,

**Figure 3.2  Tasks and stages of the supply cycle**

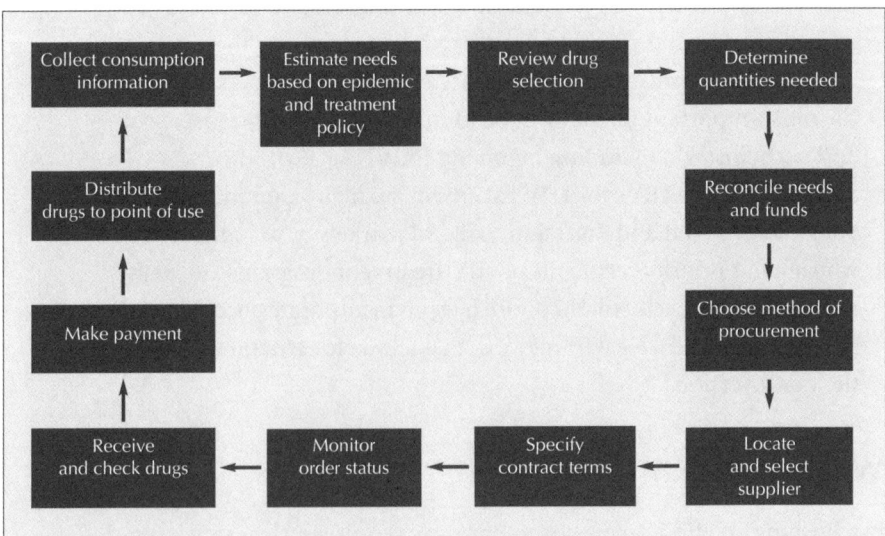

and monitoring and evaluation. All require the active cooperation of procurement and nonprocurement staff to succeed. Management support for these collaborations will also depend on good information systems and effective communication.

Multidisciplinary approaches are unusually important in dealing with the complexities of the HIV epidemic and providing medicines to combat it. Remember that failures in supply are not simply a question of interrupting the good running of programs. Interruptions in supply mean danger to patients because of the high risk of treatment failure and the possibility of developing drug resistance—and the consequent loss of health, social, and economic benefits to the country.

## Who is already carrying out these tasks?

In some countries there are agencies, institutions, and individuals with expertise and experience that the Bank could (and does) work with to achieve successful outcomes in Bank-funded HIV programs. The appropriate use of other facilities and personnel can help speed development of effective procurement systems for HIV-related medicines, saving time and scarce resources. It can also help mainstream HIV-related treatment within general provisions for health care and increase understanding of the importance of treatment within the broad context of support, care, and prevention in the HIV epidemic.

Some agencies will be able to help with specific types of products, such as medical equipment, ARVs, or HIV tests. Others will have expertise in particular elements of the supply cycle relevant to Bank-supported programs and projects. Some expertise will be available within the country or region. And some will have to be sourced internationally—for example, through existing HIV treatment or essential medicines networks, including the WHO and UNAIDS. One-off or occasional assistance may be sufficient, but some assistance may need to be recruited for ongoing involvement or cooperation to sustain a supply cycle. Assistance from others can also be found through their publications and websites, particularly from the WHO Essential Drugs and Medicines Policy, Management Sciences for Health, and UNICEF.

An assessment should be made at an early stage to find out who is already carrying out the tasks related to the supply cycle and to test whether the Bank needs to fund the setting up of new systems and personnel, the use of existing ones, or a combination of both. A preliminary mapping exercise could be used to identify different systems and personnel relevant to Bank-financed HIV procurements. The strengths and weaknesses of each one should be examined, estimating their willingness and capacity. Bear in mind that a period of rapid growth will be a feature of most HIV treatment programs during scaling up. This may strain the capacities and funding of all those who have a part in treatment delivery. It may thus have unforeseen effects on their ability to provide cooperation as programs develop.

When it is clear who can do what for Bank-funded HIV procurement in a specific country, a further assessment of the proposed procurement systems should be carried out. This may also be used as a tool for monitoring, evaluation, and replanning.[7] The assessment should cover:

- Procurement performance indicators.
- Procurement system procedures.
- Procurement system responsibilities.
- Procurement finance.
- Procurement effects on HIV treatment continuity.

Further detail of the first four items in the list can be found in Chapter 13 of *Managing Drug Supply*.[8] The fifth item should be considered as a separate part of the assessment for reasons already stated. The continuity of HIV treatment is crucial, and experience in other programs, such as the Directly Observed Treatment Short-course (DOTS) program, indicates that supply cycle failures can often be traced back to procurement difficulties. It is important that procurement personnel understand the effects of their performance on the health of people with HIV.

## Monitoring procurement results

An assessment of the initial situation should also lead to the setting up of monitoring and evaluation criteria and tools for the ongoing performance of procurement. Performance indicators and monitoring proce-

---

[7] *Managing Drug Supply*, Management Sciences for Health, in collaboration with the WHO, 2nd ed, revised, p. 180.
[8] Ibid.

**Box 3.1 Who can help in selection and quantification?**

Usually, a national HIV/AIDS council or secretariat is the central point for collecting official figures for HIV incidence and prevalence. It is also the body responsible for setting HIV/AIDS treatment policies and guidelines that will include the list of medicines considered appropriate for use in that country.

The Joint United Nations Programme on HIV/AIDS and the World Health Organization can also provide official estimates of prevalence and incidence, and model lists of products, particularly in *Guidelines for Scaling Up Antiretroviral Therapy in Resource-Limited Settings* (www.who.int/hiv/pub/prev_care/en/).

HIV/AIDS program staff with experience providing HIV treatment in target areas can provide valuable supplementary information about choosing treatment regimens acceptable to patients, minimize side effects, and support adherence. Some drugs are more acceptable than others, and patient preferences must be considered as well as cost and quality in choosing products.

National drug program staff with experience in selection and quantification of medicines should also be used as resources wherever possible since they will have detailed practical knowledge of many of the considerations and constraints that dictate product choice and their consequent effects on procurement.

Nongovernmental organizations or faith-based organizations with experience in procuring health supplies can also be a useful resource. Some of them have many years of experience in essential drugs supply. They are familiar with problematic areas such as constraints on importation and use of generics, and they are becoming more involved in the supply of HIV-related drugs and tests.

dures, responsibilities, and finance will be expected. But the relationship between these and the effectiveness of HIV treatment should also be tracked to have a full and honest picture of end results of procurement.

Monitoring typically employs four methods:

- Supervision—continual, informal monitoring of implementation and progress.
- Routine reporting of data, using a management information system.
- Sentinel sites, for more detailed reporting and monitoring of developing situations.
- Special studies to gather additional information or resolve problems.

Selection of indicators will be a local choice, depending on methods of procurement and facilities available for collecting data. Indicators should

**Box 3.2  Who can help with regulatory issues of product registration, intellectual property, and import?**

Regulatory issues in pharmaceuticals are unavoidably complex, requiring up-to-date knowledge of laws and procedures.

Registration of drugs and medical supplies, aimed at ensuring the quality, safety, and efficacy of products placed on the market in a country, is normally the responsibility of the Ministry of Health or equivalent. These requirements may also be based on quality assurance schemes or conventions applied internationally, such as:

- The World Health Organization Pre-Qualification Scheme for HIV drugs, available at mednet3.who.int/prequal/default.shtml
- The Pharmaceutical Inspection Cooperation Scheme, available at www.picscheme.org/overview/picsrole.htm
- The International Conference on Harmonization, available at www.ich.org/

Intellectual property issues are usually within the remit of the Ministry of Trade or equivalent, based on whether the country of origin and the country of import are members of the WTO and bound by the TRIPS Agreement.

Enforcement of importation regulations is generally a customs responsibility, in cooperation with other trade departments, over application of import taxes and tariffs within the framework of any relevant international trade agreements.

Procurement planning must therefore include an in-country assessment of the regulatory situation, to ensure that the products chosen for HIV programs are legitimately on the market in that country or can be imported. Anomalies within and between different sets of regulations are not uncommon and accurate factual information should be sought and relied on rather than assumptions. Costs incurred by registration, import, or other regulatory requirements are included in budgetary planning.

Legal expertise will be required to address any problematic situations that may arise. Personnel within the relevant ministries should also be identified to provide assistance in clarifying legal requirements and procedures. Experts within the country, region, or international sphere also need to be identified to provide advice and information.

The World Health Organization's Essential Drugs and Medicines Policy (WHO/EDM) can offer much expertise and information on drug registration, quality assurance, and regulatory frameworks for medicines. Nongovernmental organizations such as Médicins Sans Frontières (www.accessmed-msf.org/index.asp) and noncommercial suppliers such as the International Dispensary Association (www.ida.nl/engels/ida.html) can assist with practical experience of these matters in many countries. Considerable information specific to the intellectual property aspects of pharmaceuticals can be found on the website of the Consumer Project on Technology at www.cptech.org/ip/health/.

## Box 3.3  Who can help with procurement?

A number of agencies may be able to assist with procurement. As mentioned above, they may be in-country, regional, or international agencies, able to offer useful advice and guidance or to help with actual procurement of particular goods.

Some U.N. agencies, such as the United Nations International Children's Emergency Fund (UNICEF) and the WHO, have long experience in procuring health goods and have established procedures and policies to deal with this. They can provide lists of products, indicate sources, and assist in price comparisons, as can Médicins Sans Frontières and the International Dispensary Association (IDA). For example:

- WHO Drug Price Information: www.who.int/medicines/organization/par/ipc/drugpriceinfo.shtml
- WHO HIV Test Kit Bulk Procurement Scheme, available to government and nongovernment HIV programs, planned to expand to CD4 and other tests in the future: www.who.int/bct/Main_areas_of_work/BTS/HIV_Diagnostics/HIV_Diagnostics.htm
- UNICEF list of PMTCT-Plus drug prices: www.unicef.org/supply/
- Médicins Sans Frontières pricing guide for antiretrovirals for developing countries: www.accessmed-msf.org/prod/morepublications.asp?catid=1&subcatid=191&status=188
- IDA product list: www.ida.nl/engels/ida.html

Nongovernmental organizations' supply networks, particularly those of faith-based organizations, may be a viable alternative in some countries where these organizations have a role in the Bank-supported HIV programs. Some countries have efficient, experienced, and well-run church–health association supply schemes, for example in Uganda (Joint Medical Stores), Kenya (MEDS), and Ghana (CHAG).

be chosen judiciously to provide realistic information to those who need it for management and planning. Routine reporting and the use of sentinel sites should also be chosen in a way that makes it possible to track the effects of procurement on the overall goals—appropriate and effective treatment for people with HIV—in other words, the right medicines, of the right quality, at reasonable price, at the right quantities, where they are needed and at the right times.

## Box 3.4 Who can help with storage and distribution?

Systems for storage and distribution of medicines must achieve the following:

- Constant supplies of medicines.
- Medicines in good condition until they reach the patient.
- Losses due to spoilage and expiry minimized.
- Theft and fraud prevented.
- Accurate inventory records maintained.
- Rational storage points organized for timely delivery, quality maintenance, and security.
- Transportation resources used efficiently.
- Accurate and appropriate information collected for forecasting drug needs.

Existing public health storage and distribution networks may be used for HIV treatment goods if they can meet performance requirements, and have enough capacity (on start-up and later during scaling up). Information on local experiences with existing networks should be gathered from end users (health facilities) to assess whether they would be a viable option for the procurement and supply needs of Bank-funded HIV programs. If not, alternative means will need to be found—or capacity and management improved to bring systems up to the required standards.

Private distribution networks run by commercial companies may also be a viable alternative, if companies understand the importance of continuity of HIV supply and have facilities that ensure quality maintenance and security throughout the distribution chain.

# 4

## Product Selection, Quantification, and Quality Assurance

Rational selection of essential drugs for the treatment of HIV/AIDS is the first and most important step in achieving effective therapy against HIV and related illnesses. The cornerstone of any public health approach to combating these diseases is an efficient and effective drug supply system based on the selection of a standard list of essential drugs.

Quantification involves estimating the quantities of each commodity needed for procurement and deciding how much to buy. ARVs, test kits for HIV/AIDS, and related supplies can be quantified by various standard methods, using reliable data about past consumption, current need, and possible future expansions of services.

Quality assurance of pharmaceuticals is of paramount importance in procurement for HIV/AIDS programs. Drugs used in any medical intervention must be safe, effective, and consistent in quality. Failure to meet these requirements will lead to more treatment failure, greater drug resistance, and wasted resources. It will also make procurement more difficult—comparisons of suppliers and prices of products from different sources can be done only if they are of equivalent quality and effectiveness.

### Product selection

Procurement agencies and staff do not function in a vacuum. They are either directly or indirectly aided by technical agency staff, and in resource-poor situations functional capacities are often blurred. Baseline knowledge of therapeutic goals empowers procurement and technical staff to become better managers and better decisionmakers.

This chapter summarizes the goals, principles, and options for therapy in HIV and related conditions, providing the basis for selecting drugs. A model list of ARVs, based on World Health Organization (WHO) and Joint United Nations Programme on HIV/AIDS (UNAIDS) recommendations, is at the end of the chapter. A list of opportunistic diseases and drug regimens can be seen at: www.unaids.org/publications/documents/impact/opportunistic/opportue.pdf

Procurement should be based on the most up-to-date lists available locally, using national lists where they exist and local expertise to achieve the best selection for local program needs.

## Goals of therapy for HIV/AIDS

ART of HIV will be used in a variety of situations. Infected adults and adolescents represent the largest group of patients, of course. But treatment is also needed for younger children infected through blood-borne transmission or sexual activity. It is needed for infants infected during birth or breastfeeding. It is needed for health and emergency workers infected through exposure to bodily fluids of infected patients. And it is needed for victims of sexual or other assaults.

ART is aimed at reducing the plasma viral load as much as possible, for as long as possible. It does this by preventing the replication of the virus in an infected person's cells. ART does not kill virus particles, but these particles are short-lived and the number of particles (the viral load) drops quickly if reproduction is blocked. In principle, ART should be started before the immune system is severely damaged. But experience has shown that even patients with very low CD4 counts who have received no previous ART can recover with adequate treatment and support.

Successful treatment for HIV and related health problems will result in the following:

■ Reduction of HIV-related morbidity and mortality—less sickness and longer lives.

- Improved quality of life—with effects for the individual, family, and society.
- Restoration or preservation of immunological functions—enabling people to defend themselves against new infections and recover more quickly from illness.
- Maximum and durable suppression of viral replication—with HIV viral loads reduced as far as possible for as long as possible, benefiting the infected individual and reducing the chances of transmission to others.

These goals can be achieved through the following:

- Preventing opportunistic illnesses from HIV infection.
- Preventing transmission of the virus, whether through physical measures or specific drug treatments.
- Treating any HIV-related medical condition, or any other illness that causes particular problems for people with HIV, including tuberculosis, sexually transmitted infections, malaria, other infections, and anemia.

The clinical goals for each individual will include the following:

- Improved overall health status.
- Viral load reduced to less than 20 cells per cubic milliliter, CD4 within normal range (550–1,400 cells per cubic milliliter).
- Prevention or reduction of drug-resistant strains of HIV, tuberculosis, and drug-resistant strains of other diseases.
- Reduction and control of drug side effects and support for adherence.
- Reduced need for medical interventions and support.

### *Principles of treatment for HIV/AIDS*

The practical application of treatment varies according to the situation of the patient and the resources available. Adequate food and water supplies and the basic means of ensuring hygiene, comfort, and support are also key elements in achieving good therapeutic outcomes.

Whatever the treatment regimen, committing and adhering to treatment are required. The regimen should thus take convenience into account, as well as the patient's tolerance of both the regimen and the drugs. This is particularly important for the long-term (lifelong) treatment required for highly active antiretroviral therapy (HAART) in adults or children. Adherence failures lead to treatment failure and the development of drug resistance, which then require the patient to change to a different regimen using alternative drugs that are likely to be more expensive or that may not even be available. Adherence failures are more likely if regimens are too complicated, if patients are worried or forgetful about their drugs, or if they are depressed or lacking support. Simpler regimens and fewer side effects will therefore encourage greater adherence and more successful treatment outcomes.

The risk of drug resistance is reduced through a combination of three or four drugs with different mechanisms of action. Such combinations should enhance activity against the virus without increasing toxicity to the patient. Testing for resistance to ARVs should be considered, particularly if therapy fails. But it is unlikely to be available in low-resource situations for some time. New programs for ART should include measures to track the appearance and types of drug resistance.

### Treatment of opportunistic infections and other health problems

Even when ARVs are not available, treatment of opportunistic infections can achieve a marked degree of recovery for the immune systems of many patients, if problems are treated promptly with effective drugs. These drugs will also be required when ARVs are available—to provide faster recovery from illness and increased chances of survival. Procurement for ART programs must therefore ensure that supplies of these drugs are available to support the success of the program. The same applies to drugs for pain relief, palliative care, skin problems, diarrhea, and mental health problems, such as depression. ART programs will succeed only if they address the treatment needs of patients holistically, rather than exclusively dealing with the HIV infection.

### Treatment of HIV infection in adults and adolescents

As more experience is gained, recommended drug combinations are changing rapidly for adults. In high-resource settings, HIV treatment is highly individualized to the patient's needs and preferences. In low-resource settings, there is a need to reach as many people as possible using cost-effective public health approaches. Standard treatment guidelines have thus been developed for most countries, backed by guidance from the WHO and UNAIDS, exemplified by the *WHO Guidelines on Scaling Up Antiretroviral Therapy in Resource-Limited Settings.*

A single first-line regimen and a limited number of second-line regimens should be used. But patients who cannot tolerate these should be referred for individualized care to specialist physicians. Charts of recommended first-line and second-line regimens are given in the WHO guidelines, available in full and as an executive summary: www.who.int/ hiv/ pub/prev_care/en/

Regional adaptations are also available; for example; South East Asia, at www.whosea.org/hivaids/publications.htm, and Latin America at www.paho.org/English/HCP/HCA/arv_adultos.htm (Spanish only).

In situations with restricted health resources, decisions about when to start treatment are based on the WHO's HIV disease-staging system:

- *Stage I:* HIV-positive, no obvious disease; able to do normal activities.
- *Stage II:* Mild weight loss (less than 10 percent) and minor disease symptoms (skin problems and infections, sinus infections); still able to do normal activities.
- *Stage III:* Weight loss more than 10 percent, prolonged diarrhea or fever, tuberculosis, oral leukoplakia or thrush, other bacterial infections; bedridden less than 50 percent of the day over a one-month period.
- *Stage IV:* Most other AIDS-defining illnesses; bedridden more than 50 percent of the day over a one-month period.

Table 4.1 gives WHO recommendations for initiating ART in adults and adolescents with documented HIV infection.

According to WHO guidelines, the availability of basic blood tests is therefore essential for decisions about starting treatment. If CD4 tests are not available, treatment should not be started with people who have no symptoms, since total lymphocyte counts are not reliable for such patients.

**Table 4.1 WHO recommendations for initiating ART in adults and adolescents with documented HIV infection**

---

If CD4 testing is available:

- **WHO Stage IV disease irrespective of CD4 cell count**

- **WHO Stage III disease** (including but not restricted to HIV wasting, chronic diarrhea of unknown etiology, prolonged fever of unknown etiology, pulmonary tuberculosis, recurrent invasive bacterial infections, or recurrent/persistent mucosal candidiasis) **with consideration of using CD4 cell counts < 350/mm³ to assist decision making**[1]

- **WHO Stage I or II disease with CD4 cell counts = 200/mm³**[2]

---

If CD4 testing is unavailable:

- **WHO Stage IV disease irrespective of total lymphocyte count**

- **WHO Stage III disease** (including but not restricted to HIV wasting, chronic diarrhea of unknown etiology, prolonged fever of unknown etiology, pulmonary tuberculosis, recurrent invasive bacterial infections, or recurrent/persistent mucosal candidiasis) **irrespective of total lymphocyte count**

- **WHO Stage II disease with a total lymphocyte count = 1200/mm³**[3]

---

(1) CD4 count advisable to assist with determining need for immediate therapy. For example, pulmonary TB may occur at any CD4 level and other conditions may be mimicked by non-HIV etiologies (e.g., chronic diarrhea, prolonged fever).

(2) The precise CD4 level above 200/mm³ at which ART to start has not been established.

(3) A total lymphocyte count of 1200/mm³ can be substituted for the CD4 count when the latter is unavailable and HIV related symptoms (Stage II or III) exist. It is not useful in the asymptomatic patient. Thus, in the absence of CD4 cell testing, asymptomatic HIV infected patients (WHO Stage I) should not be treated because there is currently no other reliable marker available in severely resource constrained settings.

Source: WHO. 2003. Scaling up antiretroviral therapy in resource-limited settings—Revision. Consult www.who.int/3by5/publications/documents/arv_guidelines/en/ for updates.

## Treatment of HIV infection in women with childbearing potential or who are pregnant

The WHO's recommended drugs for use with this group of patients include ZDV, 3TC, NVP, NFV, and SQV with low-dose ritonavir.[9] All of these have been widely used to treat pregnant women. EFZ is not recommended in the first trimester because of the risk of causing abnormalities in the fetus. Women must have access to effective contraceptive methods to prevent unintended pregnancies. And since non-nucleoside reverse transcriptase inhibitors or protease inhibitors can lower the blood concentration of hormonal oral contraceptives, women should be advised to use additional or alternative methods of contraception. Further advice on ART for this group of patients is in the WHO guidelines.

## Treatment of HIV infection in children

Most ARVs used to treat adults can also be used by children if the necessary drug strengths are available in appropriate pediatric doses. But some may not be usable due to a lack of suitable formulations for children. Specific research data are lacking on the effects of some other ARVs on children. A summary of pediatric drug formulations and doses is in the WHO guidelines.

## Prevention of mother-to-child transmission

Prevention of mother-to-child transmission (PMTCT) refers to specific treatment given to an HIV-infected mother just before the time of birth, and to the infant just after birth and during breastfeeding. The sole purpose of such treatment is to prevent the infant from becoming HIV-infected. This treatment can reduce prenatal transmission by up to 70%. Available regimens include zidovudine, zidovudine plus lamivudine, or nevirapine alone. Nevirapine, the lowest-cost and simplest regimen, is the treatment of choice in many PMTCT programs. Risks of short-term toxicity are low, though long-term toxicity studies are still ongoing.

---

[9] The abbreviated chemical names are used for ARVs. See table 4.2 for a list of ARVs and their alternative names.

PMTCT-plus, recommended wherever possible, also involves providing treatment for any health problems in the mother or other immediate family. This ensures that the child's survival is not compromised by the poor health of those responsible for care and ensures equitable treatment in a family.

### Post-exposure prevention

The availability of post-exposure prevention and the means for taking universal precautions (gloves, bleach, safe disposal of needles, sterilization of sharp instruments) are essential to protect the health of emergency workers who might be exposed to HIV infection in the course of their work. In the case of needle sticks or other injuries with potentially contaminated material, a standard regimen of drugs must be made available to prevent the virus from taking hold. Post-exposure prevention should also be made available to victims of sexual or other assault when the risk of HIV transmission is high. Guidance on these topics is available from the WHO at www.who.int/hiv/topics/prophylaxis/en/ and www.who.int/hiv/topics/precautions/universal/en/.

The drugs most commonly used for post-exposure prevention include zidovudine, lamivudine, and indinavir or efavirenz (except in pregnant women). A standard regimen should be available so that treatment can start within a few hours (preferably two to four hours). A minimum of two weeks and a maximum of four weeks' treatment is recommended. Referral to a specialist will be necessary if a drug-resistant HIV strain is suspected.

## How drugs should be selected for HIV-related treatment

Public health criteria for selecting ARVs and drugs for opportunistic infections focus on drugs of the greatest importance to satisfy the health needs of the majority of the population of HIV-positive people:

- The selection of drugs should be carried out by a multidisciplinary group, including representatives of the national AIDS committee or council and the national drug formulary committee, including representatives of the Ministry of Health, together with an HIV specialist doctor, an HIV specialist nurse, a pharmacist with knowledge of available HIV-related medicines, and a procurement specialist. Additional members may be co-opted on an ad hoc basis.

▪ Drugs should be identified in any printed material by their generic name, or international nonproprietary names, but abbreviated chemical names and brand names will also be used when appropriate.

▪ Drug selection should be based on predetermined criteria, as recommended by the WHO or any existing guidelines of the national drug or AIDS programs.

As with all essential drugs, emphasis will usually be placed on products containing single active drugs. But since the combination treatment of HIV usually uses three or more ARVs in fixed ratios, combination products containing two or more drugs may be desirable to reduce the "pill burden" for patients and sustain adherence to regimens. Similar considerations apply to tuberculosis drugs and other infections such as malaria, where combination treatment is necessary and adherence crucial. The disadvantages of combination products are that it is more difficult to alter doses of individual drugs in response to patient variations in reaction or side effects, and to determine which drug in the combination is responsible for a particular side effect. Patients who do not fit the standard treatment regimens will need to be referred for specialist care.

The national formulary (prescribing manual) should be updated to include the list of drugs and prescribing information considered essential for HIV/AIDS–related treatment, including ART drugs and drugs for opportunistic infections, palliative care, and cancer treatment (table 4.2). These lists should be distributed to all public health institutions. Only drugs in the manual should be available at public-sector health institutions. In exceptional circumstances, specially authorized drugs may be obtained for specific patients according to a prescribed procedure. The essential drug list should be updated annually.

***New classes of ARVs*** Research into new drugs to combat HIV is ongoing, and two new classes of ARVs are showing some promising results. Fusion inhibitors interfere with HIV's ability to enter human cells, and enfuvirtide (Fuzeon) is the first of this class to be placed on the market, but it is currently priced too high for widespread use. Integrase inhibitors interfere with HIV's ability to insert its genes in the normal DNA inside human cells.

Table 4.2 WHO first-line ARV regimens in adults and adolescents and characteristics that can influence choice

| ARV Regimen | Major Potential Toxicities | Usage in Women (In Childbearing Age or Who Are Pregnant) | Usage in TB Coinfection (1) | Availability as Three-Drug Fixed-Dose Combination | Laboratory Monitoring Requirements | Price for least Developed Countries As of June 2003 (US$/year)(4) |
|---|---|---|---|---|---|---|
| d4T/3TC/NVP | d4T-related neuropathy, pancreatitis, and lipoatrophy; NVP-related hepatotoxicity and severe rash | Yes | Yes, in rifampicin-free continuation phase of TB treatment. Use with caution in rifampicin-based regimens (1) | Yes | No | 281–358 |
| ZDV/3TC/NVP | ZDV-related GI intolerance, anemia, and neutropenia, NVP-related hepatotoxicity and severe rash | Yes | Yes in rifampicin-free continuation phase of TB treatment. Use with caution in rifampicin-based regimens (1). | Yes (3) | Yes | 383–418 |

| | | | | | |
|---|---|---|---|---|---|
| d4T/3TC/EFV | d4T-related neurophathy, pancreatitis and lipoatrophy; EFV-related CNS toxicity and potential for teratogenicity | No (2) | Yes, but EFV should not be given to pregnant women or women of childbearing potential, unless effective contraception can be ensured | No. EFV not available as part of FDC. However, partial FDC available for d4T/3TC(3). | No | 350–1,086 |
| ZDV/3TC/EFV | ZDV-related GI intolerance, anemia, and neutropenia; EFV-related CNS toxicity and potential for teratogenicity | No (2) | Yes, but EFV should not be given to pregnant women or women of child-bearing potential, unless effective contraception can be ensured | No. EFV not available as part of FDC. However, partial FDC available for ZDV/3TC. | Yes | 611–986 |

(1) See Section VIII.C (People with Tuberculosis Disease and HIV Coinfection).
(2) See Section VIII.A (Women of childbearing potential or who are pregnant).
(3) These combinations have not been pre-qualified by WHO, but could be used if assured quality formulations of proven bioequivalence are available.
(4) Source: Sources and prices of selected medicines and diagnostics for people living with HIV/AIDS, June 2003. www.who.int/medicines/organization/par/ipc/sources-prices.pdf
Source: WHO. 2003. Scaling Up Antiretroviral Therapy in Resource-Limited Settings. Consult www.who.int/3by5/publications/documents/arv_guidelines/en/ for updates.

As mentioned, combined formulations present some advantages in reducing pill burdens (the frequency and number of tablets that have to be taken each day). Some of these drugs are produced by innovator companies, such as Combivir (ZDV+3TC), Trizivir (ABC+3TC+ZDV), and Kaletra (LPV+r). Generic producers are also beginning to provide them, either as copies of innovator combinations or as alternatives based on recommendations for regimens in low-resource countries—for example, Triomune (NVP+d4T+3TC). Some are available only in one combination of dosage, but others are available in two or three different dose ratios to allow more flexibility in prescribing them for individual patients. Producers are researching further possibilities with the aim of making most treatments conform to a twice-daily or even once-daily regimen, which will greatly aid adherence.

## Product quantification

It is important to realize that in situations where the HIV/AIDS epidemic or responses to it are expanding, careful judgment will be necessary to arrive at the correct quantities of each commodity needed for procurement and to decide how much to buy. Underestimates will deprive people of necessary treatments or tests. Overestimates may waste resources if limited-shelf-life products expire unused, especially as treatment protocols and diagnostic preferences change.[10]

### Quantification methods

Three methods can be used for quantification (table 4.3):

■ The *usage* (consumption) method relies on past use (consumption) records to estimate future need, adjusted for stockouts, expiration of overstocked items, and projected changes in utilization. Good for

---

[10] The WHO manual *Estimating Drug Requirements: A Practical Manual* (WHO/DAP 1995) provides a detailed explanation of the steps and calculations required for drug quantification. For quantification methods for HIV tests see *Commodity Management in VCT Programs: A Planning Guide.* 2002. Management Sciences for Health (RPM Plus and Family Health International, www.msh.org/projects/rpmplus/VCT_Planning_Guide.pdf).

## Table 4.3 Quantification methods

| Method | Advantages | Disadvantages |
|---|---|---|
| **Usage (consumption) or adjusted usage (adjusted consumption)** | Less complicated, easier to calculate estimates<br><br>Usually more accurate, if based on accurate statistics and conformity to treatment guidelines | Difficult to adjust for anticipated changes in demand and use<br><br>May perpetuate irrational use of medicines and laboratory tests<br><br>Insufficient on its own if the demand situation is changing |
| **Morbidity** | May be the best alternative for new drugs or programs with no historical use, such as new ART programs<br><br>Can promote rational use of medicines and laboratory tests by:<br><br>– Prompting periodic evaluation of needs and not relying simply on previous usage<br><br>– Encouraging use of current treatment guidelines | Time-consuming and more complex<br><br>Standard treatment guidelines may not be adhered to<br><br>Requires reliable and up-to-date morbidity and patient attendance records<br><br>Requires sound professional judgment by target treatment population because:<br><br>– Actual prevalence figures may be much higher than seroprevalence figures<br><br>– Availability and accessibility of ARVs may encourage more patients to come forward for testing and treatment<br><br>– Some HIV/AIDS patients may refuse ART |

established health facilities with predictable needs, this method cannot be used for new or rapidly changing situations.

- The *adjusted usage* (adjusted consumption) method uses data from other facilities, regions, or countries, adjusted or extrapolated to the specific situation on the basis of population coverage or service level. This method can be used when other methods are unreliable or when starting up new facilities or services. Data can be taken from comparable HIV treatment and procurement programs, or from producers or suppliers willing to share their experience and assist in establishing delivery schedules.

- The *patient morbidity–standard treatment method* estimates the need for specific drugs, based on the expected number of attendances, the prevalence or incidence[11] of diseases, and standard treatment guidelines for the health problems that are to be treated. For HIV testing programs (such as voluntary counseling and testing facilities), HIV seroprevalence is used to estimate the need for HIV test kits (the HIV seroprevalence method). This is useful for estimating requirements for new programs, but seroprevalence figures in many countries seriously underestimate the actual prevalence of HIV. So they should always be cross-checked locally and with the UNAIDS country estimates at: www.unaids.org/Unaids/EN/Resources/epidemiology.asp

All these methods are based on data for the actual (or projected) use of health services. Their purpose is to ensure that health services have adequate drug supplies to treat their caseload of patients. The quantities estimated by these methods are less than would be needed to treat all illness in the population, which could in theory be calculated from population-based morbidity data, except that:

- The necessary population morbidity data are rarely available, and can also be difficult or costly to collect.
- Not all morbidity results in demand for health services.

---

[11] *Prevalence* is an indication of how many people in a specific population have a disease, often shown as a percentage of the population; *seroprevalence* indicates how many people have had a positive HIV test, which is often only a proportion of the actual prevalence in most countries. *Incidence* indicates how many new cases of a disease arise within a period of time, often shown as a number of people per year or month.

- The extent to which demand can be met is itself limited by the availability of health services.

The basic principles of the methods, summarized here, all require that:

- The drugs to be included should already have been selected for each type of facility whose requirements are being estimated.
- There is a consensus on the appropriate use of these drugs. For the morbidity method, as will be explained later, this consensus is explicitly formulated in standard treatment protocols.

A suggested list of common HIV-related health problems, and the drugs and products most commonly required for their diagnosis and treatment, is outlined earlier. Many countries already include such information within national HIV prevention and treatment guidelines.

### Consumption method

In the consumption method, the most accurate inventory records of past consumption are used to calculate the procurement quantities for each commodity. The method involves a sequence of arithmetical calculations shown in table 4.4. First gather together the information about each product for items 1–5, then work out the answers to items 6, 7, and 8, as indicated, to find out how much of that product to order.

### Adjusted usage (consumption) method

This starts from examining existing consumption of the drugs in question, based on a comparison with "standard" health facilities, which are already functioning and have a reasonably representative workload, acceptable drug supply, and rational prescribing and consumption. The drug consumption of the standard facility or facilities is reviewed. And for any drug whose consumption is considered inappropriate, the quantity is adjusted upward or downward to an appropriate level.

The adjusted quantities of drugs used per standard facility are converted into standard quantities per 1,000 treatment episodes for each health problem. These are then used to estimate the drug quantities required for each facility of the type concerned, according to its expected number of treatment episodes, as in the previous method.

**Table 4.4  Calculating procurement quantities**

| 1 | Average monthly usage | Um | Calculate this from: total usage (including wastage or other losses) *divided by* the period of usage time in months (such as 12 months), *minus* any stockout periods calculated as parts of a month (a 36-day stockout is 1.2 months). |
|---|---|---|---|
| 2 | Procurement period | PP | The number of months between orders. HIV test kits and some ARVs have short expiration dates—they will need to be ordered more frequently than products with longer shelf lives. |
| 3 | Lead time | Lt | The number of months between placing an order and receiving the product ready for use. If it is a new product, the supplier's estimated lead time will have to be relied on, but later orders should also rely on experience with previous orders. |
| 4 | Stock in inventory | Si | Stock already on the shelf and having expiration dates longer than the next procurement period. For a new program or a new product, this figure will be zero. |
| 5 | Stock on order | So | Stock already ordered but not yet received (including back orders, if any). For a new program or a new product this figure will be zero. |

| 6 | Safety stock | $SS = Um \times LT$ | Stock held to protect against stockouts (also called emergency stock). The minimum SS is: average monthly usage Um *multiplied by* the lead time Lt. But each program will have to determine what quantity to keep beyond this, depending on reliability of delivery and whether use is stable, increasing, or decreasing. |
| 7 | Maximum stock level | $Smax = SS + (Um \times PP)$ | Average monthly use Um *multiplied by* the procurement period PP and *added to* the safety stock SS. Total stock levels should not exceed this level. |
| 8 | Quantity to order | $Qo = Smax - (Si + So)$ | Stock in inventory Si *added to* stock on order So and *subtracted from* the maximum stock level Smax. If the product is supplied in packs of set quantities, such as 1,000 tablets or 100 HIV tests, you can calculate the number of packs from the quantity to order Qo *divided by* the quantity in the packet, if this is known. It is best to state the total quantity required and to use only the number of packs (boxes, bottles) if one has accurate information from the supplier. Confusion over quantity at the order stage can lead to serious problems later. |

## Morbidity method

The morbidity method requires data on the number of episodes of each health problem treated at health facilities and incorporates the standard treatment schedules used for each health problem to project the need for drugs and other supplies. Practitioners who plan to undertake a morbidity-based quantification are strongly advised to consult the WHO manual *Estimating Drug Requirements: A Practical Manual* (see box 4.1) for a more detailed discussion of the steps in this type of quantification.

The morbidity method requires a list of common health problems, an essential drugs list that includes therapy for the problems, and a set of standard treatments for quantification purposes (based on either average current practices or "ideal" treatment guidelines). For many health problems there are often alternative treatments, so an estimate must be made of the percentage of each regimen used for a particular problem.

For HIV-related health problems and diagnostic needs, national morbidity data should be consulted, combined with local information from health facilities that serve people with HIV, and this must be cross-checked with UNAIDS epidemiological data for the country at www.unaids.org/Unaids/EN/Resources/epidemiology.asp. Standard treatment guidelines for HIV-related health problems should also be consulted to arrive at a list of common health problems and the diagnostic or treatment proposed for each.

Morbidity-based quantification starts from two sets of data:

- The number of episodes of each health problem treated by the type or types of facilities for which drug requirements are to be estimated.
- Average standard treatment schedules agreed to for each health problem defined.

The quantity of drugs dispensed as standard treatment for each health problem, multiplied by the number of treatment episodes of that problem, provides the total quantity of drugs required for that problem. For long-term treatments, such as those involving ARVs, drug quantities should be based on a standard period of time, such as a month, which can then be used to estimate amounts needed per procurement period.

$$\left.\begin{array}{l}\text{Quantity of the drug}\\\text{specified for a standard}\\\text{course of treatment}\end{array}\right) \quad \times \quad \left(\begin{array}{l}\text{Number of treatment}\\\text{episodes of the health}\\\text{problem}\end{array}\right)$$

= Total quantity of a drug) required for a given health problem

This is repeated for each health problem and its corresponding drugs. When a drug is used for more than one health problem, the respective totals are added together to obtain the total quantity required. These quantities may then be divided by the total number of treatment episodes of all kinds, expressed in thousands, to give the average drug requirements per 1,000 treatment episodes.

---

### Box 4.1  Useful references for quantification

- Management Sciences for Health (MSH). 1997. *Managing Drug Supply, 2nd Edition 1997.* West Hartford, CT: Kumarian Press. Available from Kumarian Press ISBN 1-56549-047-9, www.kpbooks.com (reduced price for developing country purchasers).

- UNAIDS/WHO. 1999. *Operational Characteristics of Commercially Available Assays to Determine Antibodies to HIV-1 and/or HIV-2 in Human Sera.* Report 11. Geneva: UNAIDS/WHO.

- WHO/CDC/UNAIDS. 2001. *Guidelines for Using HIV Testing Technologies in Surveillance: Selection, Evaluation, and Implementation.* n.p.: UNAIDS/WHO.

- WHO/EDM. *Estimating Drug Requirements—A Practical Manual* (WHO/DAP, 1995, 158 p.) available on CD-ROM WHO Medicines Bookshelf version 3.0–2002; Essential Drugs & Medicines Policy, WHO, Avenue Appia 20, 1211 Geneva 27, Switzerland; e-mail medmail@who.int to obtain a copy.

- Walkowiak, H., and M. Gabra. 2002. *Commodity Management in VCT Programs: A Planning Guide.* Management Sciences for Health (RPM Plus) and Family Health International. Available at www.msh.org/projects/rpmplus/ VCT_Planning_Guide.pdf

### Key principles of quantification

Use two methods of quantification to check your estimates.

- For a new service or intervention, include extra supplies in the first procurement to fill the pipeline—that is, to provide enough inventory for work to commence and also to continue until the second procurement.
- For services or interventions that are expanding (such as scaling up ART), include the proposed rate of expansion in your calculations.
- Ensure that quantification of all products follows clear rules about statements of quantity—generally, the quantities of medicines should be stated in actual numbers of capsules and tablets, milliliters of liquid medicines, or numbers of ampules or vials of a stated strength of injection. Do not allow use of indeterminate amounts; for instance, boxes, bottles, or packets, since these can vary considerably, even from the same suppliers.
- Include lead times in calculations—the amount of time between deciding to order and having new supplies available for use.
- Adjust estimates for losses and waste.
- Monitor consumption patterns and be alert of countries' tendency to err on the conservative side.
- If funds are limited, set priorities for the most important products, using the vital-essential-nonessential categorization system.[12]

## Quality assurance and supplier selection

This section introduces nonexperts to the complexity of pharmaceutical quality control and regulation.[13] It is not intended as a technical manual for evaluating or analyzing medicines, functions performed in accord

---

[12] Vital (you cannot do your work without them), essential (products you would routinely expect to use in your work), or nonessential (helpful to have but the work can be done without them).

[13] *Quality assurance* is a broad term covering all the totality of arrangements ensuring that medicines are of the quality required for their intended use. It includes compliance with good manufacturing practice and quality specifications, following principles of good distribution practice and other factors.

with detailed scientific and technical procedures. The terms and examples have been somewhat simplified for illustrative purposes.

Many reliable manufacturers, both innovator and generic companies, can offer quality products, some at lower cost. The aim for procurement is sustained, consistent, and acceptable quality, rather than high or better quality—terms that are impossible to quantify. Procurement must therefore aim at selecting the right medicines, at the lowest possible cost, ensuring that quality is maintained throughout the chain of supply from producer to patient.

Substandard products appear on the market for many reasons. Cost savings can be attempted at the expense of quality, especially when pharmaceuticals have been produced exclusively for export. But even the best quality assurance systems do not prevent occasional production failures. Adhering to good manufacturing practices during production and complying with requirements for quality specifications is aimed at preventing this. Counterfeit products—which may contain the wrong ingredients, too little active ingredient, or no active ingredient, or may be in fake packaging—are deliberately put on the market with intent to deceive. Note that generic copies of innovator products, if produced in compliance with existing laws, are not fakes, but they may not be of good quality in some cases.

Procurement must include appropriate measures to ensure the quality of products and that the national competent authorities have the capacity to enforce respective laws and regulations to prevent fake or substandard medicines from reaching end users—the patients. But official national requirements designed to ensure the quality of medicines are not the same worldwide. Some countries have the expertise and capacity to rigorously enforce regulation. But regulatory approval of medicines in other countries does not always guarantee compliance with quality standards.

---

Quality control in this context involves only some measures taken by the manufacturer. It is the part of good manufacturing practice concerned with (a) sampling, specifications, and testing and (b) organization, documentation, and release procedures ensuring that all necessary operations are completed and that materials are not released for use, nor products released for sale or supply, until their quality has been judged satisfactory.

From *WHO Expert Committee on Specifications for Pharmaceutical Preparations,* 36th report, TRS 902 (WHO 2002).

The systematic approach for procurement of these products should include, as with any other pharmaceutical procurement, the following measures:[14]

- Prequalifying suppliers and products through careful selection based on evaluation of individual product dossiers and compliance with good manufacturing practices.[15]
- Specifying detailed supplier conditions in the contract, including technical specifications.
- Monitoring quality, including laboratory testing.
- Installing systems for continuous evaluation of supplier performance.

For HIV/AIDS-related medicines, this systematic approach has to be applied widely because medicines are usually relatively new with no publicly available quality control standards, analytical methods, or reference standards.[16] Quality control methods to ensure quality of these products therefore, depend largely on the original methods introduced and validated by the manufacturers of these single-source or limited-source products.

---

[14] For detailed guidance, programs should follow reference manuals such as the following:
- UN Harmonized prequalification procedures for pharmaceutical suppliers: "Model QA System for Organizations Involved in Pre-qualification, Procurement, Storage, and Distribution of Pharmaceutical Products," (WHO 2002).
- *Managing Drug Supply: The Selection, Procurement, Distribution, and Use of Pharmaceuticals,* Second edition, (MSH/WHO 1997).
- *Procurement of Health Sectors Goods,* (World Bank 2000, revised February 2001, March 2002, March 2003).
- *Operational Principles for Good Pharmaceutical Procurement* (Interagency guidelines), (WHO/EDM/PAR/99.5).
- *Marketing Authorization of Pharmaceutical Products with Special Reference to Multisource (Generic) Products. A Manual for a Drug Regulatory Authority,* Regulatory Support Series, No. 5 (WHO/DMP/RGS/98.5) (WHO 1999).
- *Guiding Principles for the Evaluation of Manufacturers for the Procurement and Sourcing of Pharmaceutical Products,* (WHO 2001).

[15] *Operational Principles for Good Pharmaceutical Procurement* (Interagency guidelines), (WHO/EDM/PAR/99.5).

[16] Reference standards—internationally approved, standardized for purity of active pharmaceutical ingredients (chemicals that carry the main biological activity of the drug. Usually the "generic" names of the drugs designate respective active pharmaceutical ingredient. In case of amoxicillin the active pharmaceutical ingredient is amoxicillin but tablets also contain other chemicals), which can be used for laboratory quality control of pharmaceutical products.

## Multisource pharmaceutical products

Multisource pharmaceutical products are those available from a wide range of manufacturers worldwide.[17] Usually, they are well-established products with a long history of use, with publicly available quality standards and reference materials to facilitate quality assessment. They may be marketed under their international nonproprietary name or with their own brand (trademark) name.

Multisource pharmaceutical products should be pharmaceutically equivalent to the innovator product—containing the same amount of the same active substance in the same dosage form. If they are also proven therapeutically equivalent, they are interchangeable. This is verified by different studies depending on the product and dosage form:[18]

■ Clinical studies using volunteers or patients (*in vivo*) have to answer the question: Do the test drug and the innovator have the same blood (urine) concentration or clinical effects? (These are studies of bioequivalence, comparative clinical pharmacodynamics, or comparative clinical trials.)

■ Laboratory studies (*in vitro*) have to answer the question: Do solid oral forms release the correct amount of active ingredient in a given length of time?

Some drugs used in HIV/AIDS care are well-established essential drugs with pharmacopoial specifications and reference standards, and many manufacturers produce them. Examples include trimethoprim/sulfamethoxazole (for pneumonia caused by the *Pneumocystis carinii*), pyrimethamine (for toxoplasmosis and isosporidiosis), methotrexate (for AIDS-related lymphoma), and ketoconazole (for esophageal and oropharyngeal candidiasis). In this case, manufacturers should produce the products in compliance with good manufacturing practice requirements and

---

[17] In many texts multisource pharmaceutical products are called generics. But the term generic has different meanings in different settings. The international nonproprietary name should be used as the alternative to any brand name.

[18] See "When equivalence studies are necessary and type of studies required. Multisource (generic) pharmaceutical products: guidelines on registration to establish interchangeability." *Quality Assurance of Pharmaceuticals: A Compendium of Guidelines and Related Materials.* Vol. 1. (WHO 1997).

be subjected to regular independent inspections by the competent authority. The products should be assessed for compliance with reference standards, following national procedures for selection and approval of pharmaceuticals for procurement.[19]

### Single-source pharmaceutical products

Single-source pharmaceutical products are available from just one manufacturer (table 4.5). Normally this happens at the beginning of the marketing of a new drug—such as new ARVs and antifungals. And normally these products are marketed as patented drugs with a brand name (trademark).

In countries where the innovator company has been granted a patent, the company will generally be protected as a single source against the marketing of equivalent products by competitors until the patent has expired. The World Trade Organization TRIPS Agreement is expanding the number of countries where pharmaceutical patents are enforced. But as discussed earlier, the TRIPS Agreement includes mechanisms that allow procurement authorities to obtain generic versions of medicines even while patents are in effect. And these mechanisms are particularly appropriate for HIV/AIDS.[20] A voluntary license may also be secured from the patent holder.

### Limited-source pharmaceutical products

Some countries had no pharmaceutical product patents before the TRIPS Agreement. For these countries, various transition periods were introduced depending on the economic status of the country and the previous patent situation. So, there are generic versions of recent innovator products available in some markets where patent protection was or is to be introduced during the transition period—products imported or locally manufactured by companies other than the innovator one (see table 4.5). This is the case in countries with manufacturing capacity, such as Argentina, China, India,

---

[19] "Marketing Authorization of Pharmaceutical Products with Special Reference to Multisource (Generic) Products. A Manual for a Drug Regulatory Authority." Regulatory Support Series, No. 5 (WHO/DMP/RGS/98.5) (WHO 1999).

[20] See "Globalization, TRIPS, and Access to Pharmaceuticals." *WHO Policy Perspectives on Medicines*, No. 3, 2001.

## Table 4.5 Multisource and single- and limited-source products

|  | Multisource products | Single-source and limited-source products |
|---|---|---|
| Patent status | Well-established products with long history of use, off patent | Recent products, still under patent in many countries Difficult-to-produce products Products without commercial interest |
| Number of existing manufacturers | Many, worldwide | The innovator manufacturer A few generic companies |
| Existing public information and standards for quality control | Yes, information available in official compendia and Guidelines for Evaluation[24] | Not available Generic manufacturers develop their own specifications |
| Existing therapeutic experience | Yes, long experience of well-documented use of products from different sources | Experience is limited in case of time and sources of products |
| Examples of HIV/AIDS–related drugs | Trimethoprim/ sulfamethoxazole Ketoconazole Methotrexate | ARVs Amphotericin B |

Mexico, Spain, and Thailand,[21] where products such as ARVs, fluconazole, ciprofloxacin, cephalosporins, or other recent anti-infectives are being produced for treatment of patients with HIV/AIDS. Since these products are not covered by patents in the country of production, they can also be legally exported by generic manufacturers to other countries where the products have not been patented—or they can be legally imported and used.

Because the most recent of these products do not yet have internationally recognized pharmacopoeial monographs that can provide public standards for comparison of chemical equivalence and impurities,

---

[21] Spain's and Thailand's changes of patent laws were prior to TRIPS signature.

independent evaluation of the quality of these products is more difficult. WHO guidelines do not cover all necessary aspects of evaluation of these noncompendial active ingredients. So, the WHO makes references to other international guidelines, such as the International Conference on Harmonization, where appropriate.

Evaluation of quality therefore cannot be done in the exact same fashion as for multisource, established products. Special attention should go to the assessment process of the product dossier to ensure that all information needed for assessing the quality of the products is presented by the manufacturer. But because the assessments are carried out by teams of highly qualified regulators representing both developed and developing countries, these issues have been handled with a rigor that ensures quality of the products prequalified.

For some drugs, documentation of therapeutic equivalence between the reference product and the generic one, using *in vivo* bioequivalence studies, is considered especially important because of the seriousness of the condition, and the complicated pharmacokinetic and physicochemical properties. This is also a key factor in the case of fixed-dose combinations.[22] So, when selecting the products prior to purchase, it is very important to request and evaluate bioequivalence studies if these are needed for that product and dosage form.[23,24] Even if properly done bioequivalence studies exist, one of the key elements is that the drug used in the studies is essentially the same as that used by the manufacturer.

Some products fall into the limited-source category because of reasons not linked with patents. One reason is the difficulty in production (as for amphotericin B, an old drug used to treat cryptococcal menin-

[22] Fixed-dose combinations are formulations of pharmaceutical products joining in a single dosage form two or more active ingredients, such as tablets containing zidovudine (ZDV) 300 mg + lamivudine (3TC) 150 mg + nevirapine (NVP) 200 mg. These are used in treatment of HIV/AIDS to simplify drug regimens and improve adherence.

[23] WHO. 1996. Multisource (generic) pharmaceutical products: "Guidelines on Registration Requirements to Establish Interchangeability, WHO Expert Committee on Specifications for Pharmaceutical Preparations," 34th report (TRS 863).

[24] WHO. 2002. *Guidance on Selection of Comparator Pharmaceutical Products for Equivalence Assessment of Interchangeable Multisource (Generic) Products,* Annex 11, WHO Expert Committee on Specifications for Pharmaceutical Preparations, 36th report, (TRS 902).

gitis). Another is a lack of profitability, as for drugs indicated only for tropical diseases (such as eflornithine, for sleeping sickness).

### *Procedures and standards for prequalifying suppliers*

It is recommended to have a system for prequalifying supplies or preselecting suppliers before procurement starts.[25] Experience shows that it is more practical, and cheaper, to eliminate substandard manufacturers and products at the beginning rather than after the bidding (open versus restricted or limited tender).[26] New and potentially interesting manufacturers or suppliers should always be submitted to the prequalification process at an early stage, to expand the list of potential suppliers and maintain competitive pressure.

The purpose of the initial quality assessment procedure is to evaluate whether the pharmaceutical products are manufactured in compliance with good manufacturing practices[27] and whether products meet the quality (used as a general term, also covers elements of safety and efficacy) requirements established.

A broad-based procurement committee comprising managers and technical staff, including quality assurance experts with appropriate knowledge and skills, should preselect suppliers.

Global initiatives that could be of use to individual countries—like prequalification of suppliers of ARVs and other related medicines and supplies of the HIV/AIDS care package—are discussed on page 59, under "Options for countries lacking capacity to prequalify suppliers."

Dossiers and manufacturers should be reevaluated at regular intervals, with reinspections at least once every three to five years. Reevaluations should also be performed if any change in the product may have impact on the safety, efficacy, or quality of the product or if the manufacturing method or manufacturing site change.

---

[25] WHO. 1999. *Marketing Authorization of Pharmaceutical Products with Special Reference to Multisource (Generic) Products. A Manual for a Drug Regulatory Authority.* Regulatory Support Series, No.5 (WHO/DMP/RGS/98.5).

[26] Operational Principles for Good Pharmaceutical Procurement (Interagency guidelines), WHO/EDM/PAR/99.5.

[27] Procurement methods: see Chapter 5, "Procurement."

### Verification of product compliance with requirements

For generic pharmaceutical products, requirements are specified in WHO guidelines.[28,29] Product dossiers must include information on details on the product; regulatory situation; active pharmaceutical ingredient specifications with details of manufacture; finished product specifications with details of manufacture, stability, packaging, labeling, product information, and leaflet; and information on interchangeability, including bioequivalence reports when needed.[30]

For single and limited sources, when products are not described in a pharmacopoeia, the product dossier should request information on in-house quality control methods in sufficient detail for them to be replicated by another laboratory, to perform quality control (see the model dossier described above). Sufficient information about the validation of in-house methods must be provided by the manufacturer.

For innovator products manufactured and registered in countries with stringent regulatory authority, the product dossier can be a summary of the one presented to the respective authority.[31] There should be appropriate certification, as well as further evidence and explanation if the product differs in any way from the product registered in the country of origin, such as in packaging, formulation, strength, specifications, or manufacturing site.

As another part of prequalification, testing should be done to verify compliance with standards and references given. But quality control testing of samples before actual supplies take place has limited value, since test samples may differ substantially from actual supplies. It does not replace the need for post-supply random sampling and quality con-

[28] WHO. 1999. *Quality Assurance of Pharmaceuticals: A Compendium of Guidelines and Related Materials. Volume 2: Good Manufacturing Practices and Inspection.*

[29] WHO. 1999. *Marketing Authorization of Pharmaceutical Products with Special Reference to Multisource (Generic) Products. A Manual for a Drug Regulatory Authority.* Regulatory Support Series, No.5 (WHO/DMP/RGS/98.5).

[30] WHO. 2001. *Guiding Principles for the Evaluation of Manufacturers for the Procurement and Sourcing of Pharmaceutical Products.* mednet3.who.int/prequal/documents/ppdoc2.pdf.

[31] WHO. 2002. See a model of product dossier in UN Harmonized prequalification procedures for pharmaceutical suppliers: "Model QA System for Organizations Involved in Pre-qualification, Procurement, Storage and Distribution of Pharmaceutical Products." Model product dossier requirements for generic and innovator products can also be found on Web site: mednet3.who.int/prequal/default.shtml.

trol analysis, preferably as close to the patient in the supply chain as possible.

Verification of compliance with good manufacturing practices will be conducted through inspections, or through certification that involves reliance on the information supplied by the national drug regulatory authority.[32] In Bank-funded programs, adherence to good manufacturing practices in line with the WHO certification scheme is a qualification requirement. The reliability of information included in the certificates depends on the capacity and reliability of the issuing authority. The capacity of the national drug regulatory authority and national good manufacturing practices requirements vary greatly among countries (not all countries have implemented the WHO's current good manufacturing practices in full scale). So it is advisable to gather information from other reliable procurement entities, governments, and institutions already having experience with a given manufacturer.

Procurement agencies appointed to be in charge of procurement or distribution should also be prequalified as another element of a quality assurance system. Guidelines for good distribution practice can serve as a basis for prequalification,[33] including checking methods of quality assurance the agency has for selecting and monitoring its own suppliers, and arrangements made for storage of products in their bulk stores and during transport.[34]

### Options for countries lacking capacity to prequalify suppliers

Not all countries have the capacity for a prequalification system, especially for single-source or limited-source products where it is difficult to check the quality of products. (Please see the notes on registration in Chapter 5, "Procurement.")

---

[32] Including those in any of the countries that are either members of the Convention for the Mutual Recognition of Inspection in Respect of the Manufacture of Pharmaceutical Products or the International Conference on Harmonization.

[33] "Guidelines on Good Distribution Practice of Medicinal Products for Human Use" (European Commission 94/c63/03).

[34] WHO. 2003. "Guide to Good Storage Practices for Pharmaceuticals," WHO Expert Committee on Specifications for Pharmaceutical Preparations, Annex 9, 37th Report (TRS 908).

In most cases, it is strongly recommended to purchase products already prequalified by the WHO-initiated project. It is now possible to benefit from the WHO list of prequalified HIV/AIDS drugs, and it will soon be possible for antituberculosis and antimalarial drugs. Countries should request support from this project, if appropriate.

For the procurement of multisource products, some countries have developed a strict system of prequalification—such as in the Organization of Eastern Caribbean States for their annual restricted tenders or purchase through not-for-profit international procurement agencies.[35]

It will be increasingly possible to rely on procurement through international not-for-profit agencies that are gaining experience with the procurement of these products. For HIV/AIDS specifically, it is also recommended to use specialized suppliers or procurement agencies, such as the United Nations Children's Fund (UNICEF) or non-UN agencies, which could fulfill the procurement needs of HIV/AIDS medications and other items.

### Toward a consolidated prequalification system

There are various mechanisms to ensure that medicines and related products of the HIV/AIDS care package acquired by country programs are safe and effective. The WHO and other UN agencies, with the support of the World Bank, have spearheaded the Procurement Quality and Sourcing Project for prequalification of manufacturers of ARVs, antituberculosis, and antimalarial drugs. The Global Drug Facility and the Green Light Committee, both at the WHO, have mechanisms to improve country programs' access to antituberculosis drugs, while UNICEF and the United Nations Population Fund provide procurement services for purchases of drugs, laboratory supplies, condoms, and contraceptives. The WHO also prequalifies HIV test kits and sexually transmitted infection tests. This is to be extended to include monitoring tools for HIV/AIDS.

---

[35] WHO. 1997. See Country Study 18.2. *Quality Assurance in Selected Countries. Managing Drug Supply,* 2nd edition, p. 283.

## Testing and laboratory capacity

Random representative sampling and testing during implementation of the program may help to detect problems in the continuity of quality of preapproved products. It will also signal to manufacturers that periodic controls are being implemented on their products. According to Operational Principles for Good Pharmaceutical Procurement, if supplier selection is performed in an efficient way it is not necessary to carry out quality control testing on every batch in each consignment.[36] Testing can be limited to target samples to gain a "snapshot" view of variations or failures in achieving acceptable and consistent quality standards.

Full pharmacopoeia testing consumes time and money, so routine sampling should be planned for suspicious products, products failing screening tests, products from new suppliers, new products, and randomly selected samples.[37]

In all purchase contracts, the manufacturer should be asked to submit the quality control specifications and all needed information on methods used for testing, as well as the appropriate certification so that testing of their products can be carried out (Certificate of Analysis,[38] Batch Analysis Certificate[39]). This requirement is especially important for single-source or limited-source products without publicly available information on methods and specifications for testing.

Many countries routinely perform quality control tests in their national control laboratory or in subcontracted laboratories (national or regional). Regional laboratories established in WHO regions are also used for multisource products. Procurement agents would normally perform quality control as required of the products they distribute.

Not all countries possess the capacity for monitoring product quality. The WHO has a project to train national drug regulatory authorities

---

[36] WHO. *Operational Principles for Good Pharmaceutical Procurement* (interagency guidelines), (WHO/EDM/PAR/99.5).

[37] WHO. 2002. *Considerations for Requesting Analysis of Drug Samples*, (TRS N° 902). www.who.int/medicines/strategy/quality_safety/trs902ann4.pdf

[38] WHO. 2002. *Model Certificate of Analysis*, WHO Expert Committee on Specifications for Pharmaceutical Preparations, Annex 10 (TRS 902).

[39] WHO. 1997. "Model Batch Analyses Certificate." *Quality Assurance of Pharmaceuticals: A Compendium of Guidelines and Related Materials.* Vol. 1. pp. 202–04.

in judging these products in their particular conditions. Countries should contact the WHO for more information: www.who.int/medicines/ organization/qsm/orgqsm.shtml

For testing single- and limited-source products, in the short term, it is strongly recommended that countries submit samples to laboratories already participating in the WHO prequalification project, which already has the expertise for such analyses. Now working with several laboratories, the WHO is planning to publish an Expression of Interest for assessing laboratories as part of a prequalification procedure.

Local or national laboratories approved by the national drug regulatory authorities already conducting testing should be allowed to continue the testing. But these laboratory facilities should be encouraged to apply to participate in the WHO prequalification procedure for quality control laboratories and to plan for the enhancement of their capacity.

International not-for-profit procurement agencies—which have their own facilities or use laboratories meeting specified standards—and private laboratories might also be acceptable if they can prove that they meet the required standards for testing the quality of medicines. Laboratories are being accredited by private entities using International Organization for Standardization (ISO) and Organisation for Economic Co-operation and Development norms and standards. The WHO publishes a regularly updated set of guidelines on quality assurance, testing, and the safety of medicines. For the guidelines and more, consult www.who.int/medicines/organization/qsm/orgqsm.html.

# 5

## Procurement

Project teams are required, as part of project preparation and appraisal, to assess the existing and potential capacity of the project-implementing agency to administer procurement efficiently. They also assess its capacity for managing ancillary critical phases of the supply chain in project implementation and beyond. The findings facilitate the development of an action plan to strengthen the agency's capacity to administer procurement effectively and transparently as part of sound governance and good project management.

### Assessing capacity

In most cases, the implementing agencies of the Multi-country HIV/AIDS Program projects are the national AIDS control organizations or commissions, working with the ministry of health and other line ministries. In many countries these bodies might lack the capacity to forecast, procure, store, and distribute ARVs and other related medical supplies of the HIV/AIDS care package. It is therefore essential to examine the procurement capacity of the central medical stores for this category of specialized drugs and supplies before deciding on the project's procurement strategy and plan.

There is evidence that many central medical stores, particularly in Africa, are procuring ARVs on a small scale for the use of private patients or for pilot programs. But to support large-scale and sustained procurement capacity of the products of the HIV/AIDS care package, a central medical store may still require assistance in strengthening its managerial capacity and augmenting its technical capabilities, mainly those for quality assurance and product testing. Actions proposed to offset deficiencies must be incorporated as project components and funded as needed.

If the implementing agency cannot finance these activities, the project team should discuss and agree on alternative financing sources with the beneficiary (such as a project preparation fund). If the central medical store is totally deficient and poorly managed, a third alternative must be sought (such as employing a specialized procurement agency or UN agency). This agency can be required, as part of its contractual obligations, to include a training, capacity-building, and technology transfer component intended to strengthen the capacity of the central medical store.

The procurement specialist (or procurement accredited staff) assigned to the project is primarily responsible for carrying out the assessment. Aspects of the assessment dealing with financial and administrative controls should be carried out with the assistance of the disbursement or financial management specialists assigned to the project. The Bank's legal procurement team should be involved as needed for any issues related to legal aspects of the procurement.

One critical issue is decentralizing procurement of drugs and other supplies to subnational or even district agencies. For political or administrative reasons, the national government may be obliged to assign the major part of procurement to the decentralized bodies. If so, the Bank appraisal team should assess the procurement capabilities of such decentralized entities as well, reflecting their findings in the action plan for augmenting procurement capacity.

The prior review thresholds and supervision plan should respond to the characteristics of the drugs and medical supplies comprising most of the procurement of HIV/AIDS projects. It is expected that procurement packages would comprise treatment regimens with high unit costs, generating large value contracts. If the assessment qualifies the agency as high risk, alternative solutions should be recommended or actions taken to reduce that risk. No high-risk implementing agency should be managing

HIV/AIDS projects; only agencies with risk categories ranging between average and low should do so. So, prior review thresholds for medicines and medical supplies could be set no lower than $350,000, supplemented by appropriate post reviews and audits.

## Commodities that support the HIV/AIDS program

The HIV/AIDS commodities package (see figure 5.1) is more complex than other products and supplies managed in the public sector:

■ A functioning lab infrastructure is essential to support service delivery (equipment, supplies, and human resources).

**Figure 5.1  Commodities that support the HIV/AIDS program**

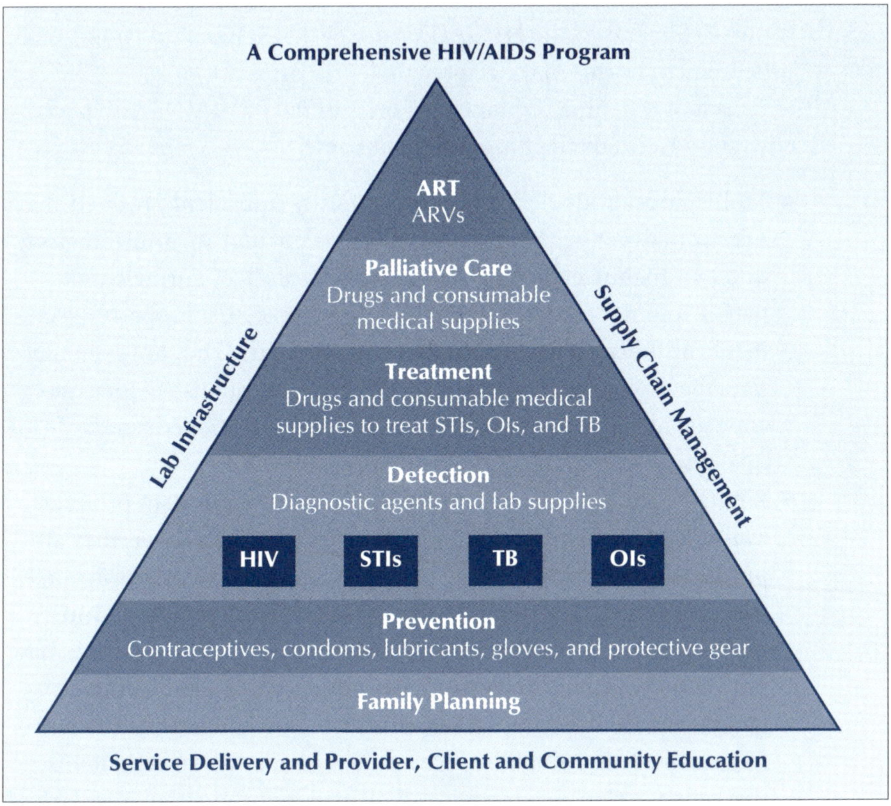

*(Reprinted with the permission of John Snow Inc./Deliver, with USAID)*

- The supply chain must be agile and responsive in changing situations, delivering products before they expire or are diverted.
- Service delivery and provider, client, and community education are in the early stages of development, unlike more established health programs.
- A set of comprehensive, interdependent services needs to be provided.
- Decentralizing interventions to the community adds to complexity of planning, coordination, distribution, and management—because the technical skills for managing these products may be lacking or insufficient.

This HIV/AIDS care package comprises three main product categories: multisource or generic products, limited-source products, and single-source products. This chapter focuses on procurement strategies and options for single-source and limited-source products. For the multisource elements of the HIV/AIDS care package, standard (traditional) procurement norms may be applied.

Each of the three product categories of the HIV/AIDS care package corresponds to a distinct procurement strategy:

- Multisource products are pharmaceutically equivalent products that may or may not be therapeutically equivalent and are available from different manufacturers. They are well established, normally off patent, and not restricted by continuing intellectual property agreements or other exclusivity market arrangements. They are generally available from a wide range of producers, have published pharmacopoeial quality standards, and have available reference standards for quality-control testing.
- Limited-source products are pharmaceutically equivalent products available from a limited number of manufacturers. Newer, they are products usually protected by patents or market-exclusivity arrangements in some countries. Pharmacopoeial quality standards and publicly available reference standards for quality control testing may not yet be available. Single-source products are generally under patent with no licensing agreements that allow other firms to manufacture the drugs. Single-source availability may be due to patents, marketing exclusivity, technical challenges of production, or a lack of economic incentives for production by other manufacturers. Some

older (off-patent) products are effectively single-source, because the lack of demand in western markets makes them unprofitable and thus unattractive to producers. Pharmacopoeial quality standards and publicly available reference standards for quality-control testing might not be publicly available.

## Planning procurement

Procurement planning is much more than choosing the procurement methods to use for various medicines, medical supplies, works, and service contracts and then scheduling the activities. The starting question is: What are the most effective procurement arrangements for achieving project objectives consistent with the Bank's Procurement Guidelines?[40]

HIV/AIDS projects do not fit the conventional approach of specific investment projects. Instead, the common characteristic of these projects is that the specific content of the operation becomes known only as the program develops, making it impractical to list the entire project's procurement needs in advance. Under these circumstances, it is advisable and desirable to identify an initial set of subprojects or components—say, for the first year—to avoid long delays in getting started. For this first period, planning can be driven by the size of the cohort of patients under each category of treatment options: voluntary counseling and testing and check-ups for HIV-positive people, HIV-positive living and survival skills, prophylaxis and treatment of opportunistic infections, ART, and prevention of mother-to-child transmission.

In the light of the difficulties in planning the number of contracts and packages and coming up with precise figures for the value of each contract, the procurement plan submitted at the time of negotiations must be updated annually. No aggregate amount for any method of procurement plan should be required in the project appraisal document or in the credit or grant agreement. But different countries might have different priorities for different treatment options depending on the availability of credit and the projected patient load. This may be established as clearly

---

[40] World Bank (1995, Revised January and August 1996, September 1997, and January 1999) *Guidelines for Procurement under IBRD Loans and IDA Credits,* Washington, D.C.

as possible during negotiations to determine the most suitable methods of procurement and to assess the existing capacity for procurement.

### Packaging contracts and scheduling procurement

Monotherapy or bitherapy with ARVs is no longer acceptable due to the high probability of drug resistance. So, different ARVs (nucleoside reverse transcriptase inhibitors, nonnucleoside reverse transcriptase inhibitors, and protease inhibitors) are used in triple or quadruple combinations, referred to as highly active antiretroviral therapy (HAART). That can make the packaging of drugs for combination treatments essential. Bidders may be required to bid for the entire combination rather than for individual drugs. Similarly, the most common opportunistic infection, tuberculosis, is treated with standard regimens of antituberculosis drugs for a fixed period. Again, the bidders may be asked to bid for complete packages of standard regimens. Procuring antituberculosis drugs in standard regimen-wise blister packs has proved very cost-effective in some settings where Directly Observed Treatment Short-course (DOTS) programs have been well supplied and managed.

One consideration in choosing whether and how to package contracts is the time when goods or services are needed. Preliminary packaging plans must first be formulated and the method of procurement to be used for each tentatively determined by the nature and size of the packages. It is then necessary to verify that these combinations will permit the goods or services to be delivered when they are needed for the project. The best way to check this is to work backward from the desired date of delivery to determine whether enough time is available to carry out the procurement steps necessary for each element. Attention should also go to related aspects of project implementation, such as manpower deployment or provision of medical equipment, envisaged or required before the delivery of the drugs can begin.

## Registering products

Countries with drug registration systems normally require that all drugs purchased through public bidding be registered locally. If product registration is necessary before drugs are allowed in, a fast-track registration process facilitated by the recipient country should be encouraged for specific categories of drugs (well-established generics, life-saving, those with no alternatives) if manufacturing facilities and active pharmaceutical ingredient sources are known and quality is assured.

Under a fast-track registration process, drugs supplied by successful bidders can be automatically allocated a preregistration status. But adequate documentation—including recent proof of registration, approval in the country of origin, stability data, and a representative sample—must be submitted as part of the bid, meeting all the qualification criteria established in the tender documents.

The registration process can be faster because suppliers are not requested to submit clinical and toxicological data to prove safety and efficacy but may rely on previously published literature—say, for dosages.

However, some particular oral solid products associated with impaired resorption profiles and a narrow therapeutic profile (anti-epileptics, rifampicine tablets, ARVs) need to be tested *in vivo* to substantiate bioavailability or even bioequivalence before registration (market entry) can be considered. The same is true for newly introduced fixed-dose combinations of these types of drugs where clinical data are not yet published and interference between active components cannot be excluded.

Another way to fast-track registration could be for the country's regulatory authority to formulate a policy that allows a product to be registered if the product originates from a country recognized as having effective pharmaceutical regulatory systems. Countries are encouraged to fast-track registration of products prequalified by the WHO-initiated project (if they are essentially the same and originate from prequalified manufacturing sites indicated in conjunction with every product on the list). The manufacturer should submit the product dossier—full or abbreviated—as stated by the national drug authority.

## Choosing procurement methods

The market situation of each product, the nature of the medicines and medical supplies, and the critical dates for delivery—are all major factors determining the choice of procurement method. Choices are restricted by the characteristics of medicines and supplies of the HIV/AIDS care package. As already noted, the majority of ARVs and some other HIV-related drugs are either single-source or limited-source products. Other drugs and commodities for opportunistic infections or for basic or palliative care may be multisource but effectively restricted to limited sources in many settings.[41] So, international (or national) competitive bidding without pre-qualification typically cannot be the preferred method of procurement. Instead, limited international bidding, direct contracting, or shopping may be the most appropriate. The key is to understand what situations are suitable for each of them.

### Limited international bidding

With this method, international bidding is conducted by direct invitation to all of the limited number of qualified suppliers and without open advertisement. This is appropriate only when a very limited number of manufacturers or suppliers can supply quality products. It is strongly recommended to validate quality of pharmaceutical products for which pharmacopoeial quality standards and publicly available reference standards for testing are not available:

- The United Nations Procurement Quality and Sourcing Project prequalifies suppliers who have been found acceptable in principle for procurement by UN agencies and provides a list of prequalified products from these suppliers. mednet3.who.int/prequal/default.shtml
- The products should have been authorized for use by the regulatory authority of a member of the Pharmaceutical Inspection Convention or an entity participating in the Pharmaceutical Inspection Cooperation Scheme. www.picscheme.org/index.htm
- The products should have been authorized for use by the regulatory authority of a member of the International Conference on Harmonization of Technical Requirements for the Registration of Pharmaceuticals for Human Use. www.ich.org/
- In exceptional circumstances, the products should have been authorized by the national regulatory authorities, when countries have a proven record of mid- to long-term use of a particular product, with established safety and efficacy, and a product dossier is available containing at least the essential information.
- The national drug regulatory authority should ensure that the source is participating in the prequalification scheme, so that the product will eventually appear under the UN project.

---

[41] Multisource products, which are restricted to limited source, do not include prevention supplies, such as condoms, lubricants, and gloves.

Bidding should be conducted following paragraph 3.2 of the World Bank's Procurement Guidelines. This is appropriate for procurement of specialized pharmaceuticals (see figure 5.2). www.worldbank.org/html/opr/procure/guidelin.html

The implementing agency would be required to have a relatively strong capacity and evaluation skills as well as solid knowledge of the sources.

### Single-source or direct contracting without competition

This method is used when the medicines or medical supplies are available from only one source. It is deemed appropriate for both small and large contract values. Drugs and related medical supplies may be single-sourced from originator enterprises at preferential prices negotiated under the auspices of international organizations, including the Joint United Nations Programme on HIV/AIDS. Procurement under such arrangements may be appropriate where equivalent nonoriginator drugs and related medical supplies at a lower price are not available from suppliers in countries where nonoriginator drugs and medical supplies are lawfully produced or marketed, or cannot be imported using flexibilities available under national intellectual property laws and regulations.

To determine the reasonableness of the price offered, beneficiaries should plan their negotiating strategy very carefully using historical prices and drug price bulletins issued periodically by the United Nations Children's Fund, Management Science for Health, and Médicins Sans Frontières (all accessible at www.who.int/medicines/organization/par/ipc/drugpriceinfo.shtml). To ensure that they obtain competitive prices, they should consult with neighboring countries on prices offered to them and inquire into pooled procurement schemes operating in the region. They should also check their own regulatory situation for the products and manufacturers proposed for procurement, particularly for patents and registrations of drugs or devices.

### Use of specialized low-cost international procurement suppliers or UN agencies

When the borrower's capacity to handle procurement is low or when the risk assessed is high, specialized bulk procurement suppliers and UN agencies acting as suppliers may be a good source of high-quality, low-cost medicines and medical supplies. The decision to hire them should be based on the needs of the implementing agency and its lack of capacity to procure the specialized goods. In those cases, they can be hired under sole-source and their use should not be limited to small quantities or small monetary value procurement.

A number of UN agencies or UN-sponsored schemes—such as the World Health Organization (WHO), the United Nations Population Fund, the Global Drug Facility Inter-Agency Procurement Services Office, and the Green Light Committee—conduct bulk or pooled procurement that guarantees quality and lower prices. These agencies, many with headquarters in Western Europe, normally charge a fixed percentage fee over the amount of the purchase. Program managers must be aware, however, of the possible limitations of these suppliers in conducting quality testing if based in countries where most drugs are protected by patents. Government authorities in these countries should establish a "regulatory review exception" to permit such testing. Even if quality tests are conducted in the manufacturing countries where generic competition is permitted, importing the drugs may remain a challenge.

### Shopping

Comparing price quotations from several local or foreign suppliers is appropriate for procuring small amounts of readily available off-the-shelf goods. To ensure competitive prices, at least three quotes must be obtained from different suppliers. Procurement under this method should comply with the requirements for quality (see page 70, under "Limited international bidding"). Purchasers should check their regulatory situation for the products and manufacturers proposed for procurement, particularly for patents and registrations of drugs or devices.

### International competitive bidding among prequalified suppliers

Under this procedure, an invitation to bid should be sent to a group of preselected manufacturers or suppliers. Because of the high expertise required and the complexities of prequalifying manufacturers of ARVs and related HIV/AIDS medical supplies, using the list of prequalified suppliers produced by the WHO under the United Nations Procurement Quality and Sourcing Project is strongly recommended. (The list is not yet comprehensive, but is regularly updated and extended.) mednet3.who.int/prequal/default.shtml

Consistent with the prerequisites under limited international bidding qualified bidders should comply with the requirements shown on page 70, under "Limited international bidding." Bidding should be conducted in accordance with the Bank's Procurement *Guidelines*. www.worldbank.org/html/opr/procure/ guidelin.html

International competitive bidding with prequalification is suitable for multisource products and essential drugs not on patent.[42] The following medicines and health supplies shall be procured using this method: condoms, sexually transmitted infection drugs, drugs for opportunistic infections, and palliative care drugs. It is appropriate for procuring large quantities. But the implementing agency must possess proven capacity to undertake procurement and satisfactory evaluation skills.

### National competitive bidding with prequalification

Because beneficiary countries may lack local manufacturing capacity to produce anything more than basic essential medicines, national competitive bidding is not usually recommended for procurement of most HIV/AIDS medicines and related commodities. It would only be recommended in those cases where there are a number of qualified local manufacturers or authorized agents of international manufacturers or licensed wholesale importers. Bidders supplying products manufactured locally must demonstrate that the quality of the local production meets WHO equivalent standards and their prices are competitive with international prices. Accordingly, they should fulfill the requirements shown on page 70, under "Limited international bidding."

National competitive bidding should be conducted in accordance with the guidelines, and the implementation unit should have satisfactory procurement experience.

---

[42] International or national bidding without prequalification are not suitable procurement methods for medicines and health supplies.

### Pooled procurement, national or regional

Pooled procurement can be national (pooling the needs of different local health systems) or regional (pooling the needs of different countries). Central Medical Stores, autonomous not-for-profit supply agencies often constituted as parastatals either under the Ministry of Health or as independent organizations, can be viable options. But they must demonstrate adequate capacity, public accountability, financial management, and quality control. Some of them may require technical assistance to strengthen their capacity, and that is consistent with the Bank's efforts to build stronger public-sector procurement systems. Since they often act on behalf of the governments, they may be better positioned to handle the complexities of the patents and drug registrations. And they can benefit from price discounts available to the public sector and from the flexibilities of compulsory licensing and parallel importing under the TRIPS Agreement.

Irrespective of the procurement method, medium and large purchases (in the range of US$200,000) should be done under the contractual provisions of the Standard Bidding Document for the Procurement of Health Sector Goods: web.worldbank.org/WBSITE/EXTERNAL/PROJECTS/PROCUREMENT/0,,contentMDK:20062738~pagePK:8426 9~piPK:84286~theSitePK:84266,00.html

### Consulting services

Hiring consulting services (say, to support voluntary counseling and testing, commission a study, hire a procurement agency[43]) should follow the procedures outlined in the applicable *Guidelines: Selection and Employment of Consultants by World Bank Borrowers.* Bank staff and staff of the implementing agencies should consult *The Consulting Services Manual,* which provides guidance on how to select and use consultants in accord with current Bank procedures. Of particular value is the section that introduces the process and various methods for selecting consultants depending on the nature of the assignment, its complexity, and the size of the project. Also

---

[43] A procurement agency can be hired by the implementing agency when there is a lack of capacity in the implementing agency to undertake procurement. The agent should follow the procurement procedures outlined in this Technical Guide. Procedures should have been included in the Credit or Grant Agreement.

helpful are the sections on the preparation of short lists, the review of documents that make up the request for proposals, and the piece on evaluating and selecting proposals and negotiating contracts with consultants: web.worldbank.org/WBSITE/EXTERNAL/PROJECTS/PROCUREMENT/0,,contentMDK:20060656~pagePK:84269~piPK:60001558~theSitePK:84266,00.html

A Standard Form of Agreement for Consultant's Services has been prepared by the Bank for use by implementing agencies when they hire UN agencies on a single-source basis for carrying out consultants' services: opcs.worldbank.org/p/themes/consultServices.htm?open

### Explanation of terms used in figure 5.2, (page 76)

**Market situation**

**On patent and available from originator and generics**—Drug or medical supply is on patent in a market or some markets, and is available from the originator—or can be lawfully produced generically in the local market or imported from a lawful source in an exporting country.

**On patent and available from originator only**—Drug or medical supply is on patent in a market or some markets, and is available only from originator.

**Off patent (multisource)**—Drug or medical supply is off patent and is available from a number of manufacturers.

**Procurement options**

**International bidding**—includes limited international bidding in cases where suppliers are limited, or international competitive bidding with prequalifications where options are multisource. Qualified national or local suppliers are included as potential bidders.

**Direct contract or single source**—only one supplier.

**Shopping**—used when contract value is small and when a bidding process would be unnecessarily expensive and resource-intensive.

**Figure 5.2  Procurement flowchart**

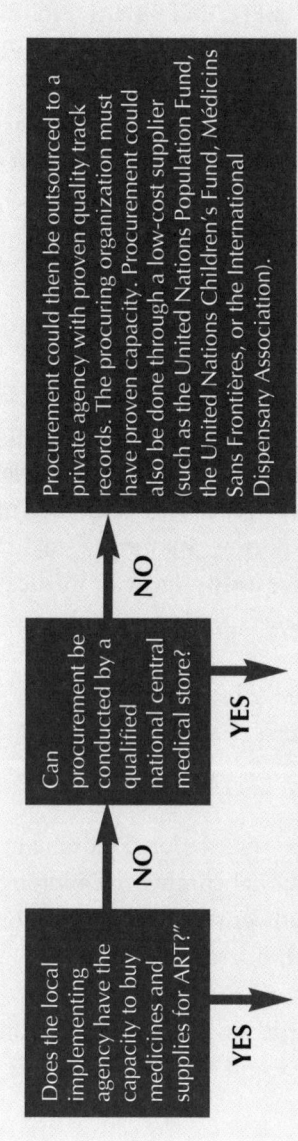

Does the local implementing agency have the capacity to buy medicines and supplies for ART?"

**YES** — **NO**

Can procurement be conducted by a qualified national central medical store?

**YES** — **NO**

Procurement could then be outsourced to a private agency with proven quality track records. The procuring organization must have proven capacity. Procurement could also be done through a low-cost supplier (such as the United Nations Population Fund, the United Nations Children's Fund, Médicins Sans Frontières, or the International Dispensary Association).

The range of medicines and medical products required for an ART program include:

| CATEGORY | ARVs | Palliative medicines | Treatment medicines | Detection supplies[44] | Prevention supplies[45] |
|---|---|---|---|---|---|
| EXAMPLES | Abacavir, Didanosine, Nevirapine, Indinavir, and so on | Anti-infective drugs, anti-cancer drugs, and so on | Antibiotics, drugs to treat tuberculosis, sexually transmitted infections, and so on | HIV detection test kits, CD4 tests, viral load tests, and so on | Condoms, lubricants, gloves, and so on |

Depending on contract value and market situation, the procurement options available are:

| CONTRACT VALUE | MARKET SITUATION | | |
|---|---|---|---|
| | On patent and available from originator and generic manufacturers | On patent and available from originator only | Off patent (multisource) |
| SMALL use SBD standard conditions of contract | Shopping | Direct contract or single source | Shopping |
| MEDIUM use SBD standard conditions of contract | Shopping or limited international bidding or international competitive bidding with pre-qualification | Direct contract or single source | Shopping or limited international bidding or international competitive bidding with prequalification |
| LARGE use SBD standard conditions of contract | Shopping or limited international bidding or international competitive bidding with pre-qualification | Direct contract or single source | Shopping or limited international bidding or international competitive bidding with prequalification |

Indicative contract values

Small: Less than $200,000    Medium: Between $200,000 and $500,000    Large: More than $500,000

44 For a more detailed explanation of the characteristics of test kits and other diagnostics please refer to Annex A of this Guide.

45 Condoms and other prevention supplies should follow customary methods of procurement. For large contract values, prequalification is highly recommended prior to international competitive bidding. In cases of lack of capacity, the project should seek the support of specialized agencies for condom procurement and distribution.

## Box 5.1  Social marketing: another way to distribute

Social marketing uses public-private partnerships to achieve a set of health objectives. It involves the application of commercial marketing concepts and tools to reach segments of the population not yet served—or not adequately served—by public and private systems. It has been used extensively in international health programs, especially for distribution of contraceptives and oral rehydration therapy kits. The United Nations Population Fund and the United States Agency for International Development have supported large social marketing programs in Africa and Asia (notably, in India, which has a large national program). World Bank projects have supported social marketing programs in Haiti and The Gambia.

Social marketing programs need to be closely coordinated with procurement to ensure that the packaging, delivery schedules, and distribution of products dovetail with promotion and marketing strategies. This may involve a service agreement in which an agency is selected competitively and contracted to provide a package of services, such as condom promotion and social marketing. If the agency is selected competitively, it would be allowed to supply condoms from its own procurement pipeline. Most agencies that are contracted as implementers, distribute condoms procured for them by donor agencies. But some agencies, including Population Services International, a U.S.-based nonprofit organization active worldwide in social marketing efforts, also procure condoms directly from manufacturers.

*Resources:* Population Services International www.psi.org; The Futures Group International www.tfgi.com/.

## Box 5.2  Useful references on procurement

- "Bank-financed Procurement Manual." July 2001. Draft. World Bank, Operations Policy and Country Services Vice Presidency, Procurement Policy and Services Group. Washington, D.C.
- "Standard Bidding Document and Technical Note: Procurement of Health Sector Goods." May 2000. Revised February 2001. World Bank, Washington, D.C.
- "Managing Drug Supply." 1997. Second Edition. Management Sciences for Health in collaboration with the World Health Organization.
- "Multi Sectoral Aids Projects (MAPs): No Product? No Program: Supply Chains—The Missing Link in HIV/AIDS Programs." Sangeeta Raja: www1.worldbank.org/hiv_aids/docs/short%20version%20-%20SCM%20and%20HIV.pdf
- "Guidelines on Procurement and Supply Management of Health Care Products (Preliminary)." January 2003. The Global Fund to Fight Aids, Tuberculosis, and Malaria.

# 6

## Pricing

The price of medications can be a significant barrier to HIV/AIDS treatment, especially for ART, a chronic treatment that requires the daily intake of a combination of pharmaceutical compounds. The coverage of health insurance in developing countries is often limited. And when drugs are purchased out-of-pocket, the price of ARVs can make a vital difference for poor people's ability to afford treatment.

Even the lowest available prices are unaffordable for most patients in the developing world, where about 3 billion people live on less than $2 a day. So many HIV-infected patients rely on the subsidized or free provision of ART by the public sector. For resource-constrained governments in poor countries, the purchase price for the pharmaceutical compounds directly affects the number of patients that can be treated. And lower prices leave more room for investments in complementary health infrastructure needed to make ART effective.

Prices for ARVs can vary substantially, with markedly different prices for the same drugs sold by the same manufacturer under similar conditions across countries. For example, in November 2002, the ARV nelfinavir was sold at $6,169 per patient per year in Switzerland, and $8,353 in Guatemala.[46]

---

[46] AIDS patients in poor countries pay higher prices than people in Switzerland for Roche's drugs: Médicins Sans Frontières press release, November 15, 2002. www.msf.org/content/page.cfm?articleid=013E49F3-B70A-4C07-881E3E214A97FFAD.

Prices can also vary substantially over time, due to improvements in production technologies and competitive dynamics. Indeed, only four years ago, triple cocktail ART was priced at $10,000–15,000 per patient per year in the United States.[47] Today, the same therapy can cost as little as $200–300, if sourced from the Indian pharmaceutical industry.[48] New— and more expensive—ARVs are needed as patients develop resistance to first-line ARVs.

## What determines drug prices?

### The pharmaceutical supply chain

To better understand the numerous determinants of drug prices, it is helpful to start by looking at the pharmaceutical supply chain (figure 6.1). Drugs generally reach patients either through retail pharmacies or through the free or subsidized provision by the public sector, which may purchase the drugs directly from the manufacturer or from a pharmaceutical wholesaler.[49]

The price of a drug when it leaves the manufacturer's factory is referred to as the manufacturer's selling price. It reflects variable production costs, fixed overheads (possibly including marketing and research and development), and profit. In addition to the manufacturer selling price, prices include (international) transport and insurance as well as applicable taxes (such as import tariffs, fees, and value-added or sales taxes). Wholesalers and retailers add their own service costs and profit margins, reflected in the final retail price. Drugs provided by the public sector are also distributed by the public sector, but these service costs typically are not reflected in the subsidized prices offered to patients.

---

[47] These are commonly accepted figures for the cost of ART in the United States. See, for example, "Drug Prices: What's Fair?" by John Carey and Amy Barrett in *Business Week*, December 10, 2001. Alternatively, retail ARV prices in the United States can be observed at a variety of pharmacies, including www.walgreens.com.

[48] See "Untangling the Web of Price Reductions—A Pricing Guide for the Purchase of ARVs for Developing Countries." (Médicins Sans Frontières, 2003, 4th Ed.). The price of triple-therapy ARV treatment is quoted as $201 per year from Hetero Drugs, $209 per year from Aurobindo Pharmaceuticals, and $295 per year from Ranbaxy.

[49] Drugs may also be distributed by the private not-for-profit sector, including nongovernmental organizations, such as Médicins Sans Frontières.

**Figure 6.1  Pharmaceutical supply chain**

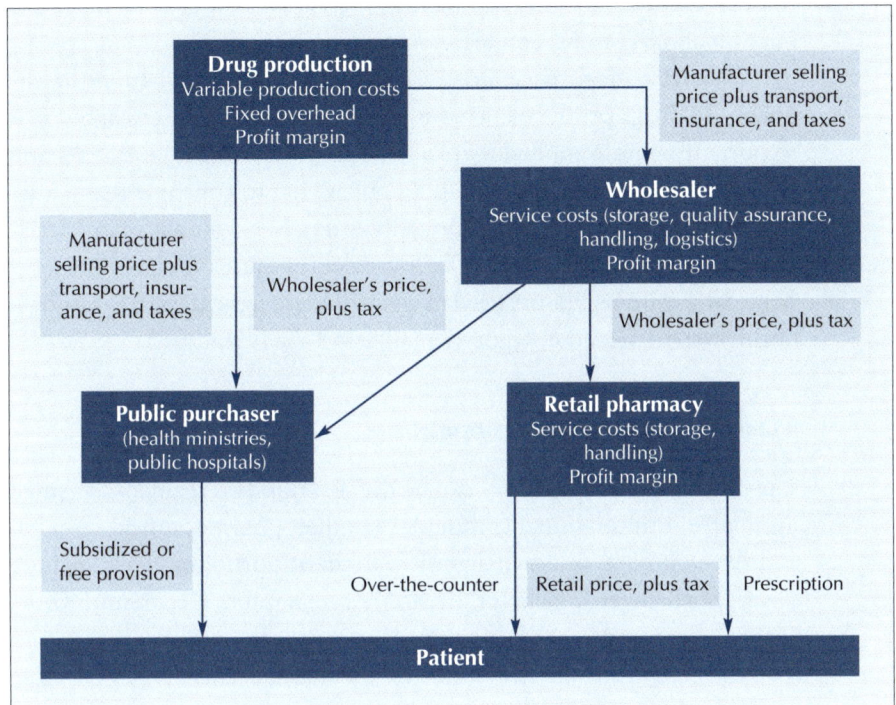

Comparing drug prices across markets or between suppliers should be based on prices observed at similar points in the supply chain. For example, a comparison of the manufacturer selling price of supplier A in one market with the retail price of supplier B in another market may say little about which manufacturer will offer a cheaper price to a public purchaser in a third market.

## *Production costs*

The production of drugs involves the transformation of active pharmaceutical ingredients into the drug formulations that have the desired medicinal properties. Economies of scale are thought to be important for the production of ARVs, so larger manufacturers may be able to produce at lower costs than smaller manufacturers. Over time and especially in the first few years after a drug has entered the market, technological improvements in the pharmaceutical manufacturing process often lead to significant cost reductions. And competitive pressures can accelerate the introduction of new production technologies.

Pharmaceutical manufacturers need to control and monitor the quality of drugs produced. That may add to production costs, but it is important because subquality products can undermine treatments and pose severe health risks. It would also be wrong to conclude that a low-cost manufacturer produces subquality drugs. For example, many developing country producers can offer low prices because they have low wage costs. So, health regulators need to ensure that drugs entering a country's health system meet the required quality and safety standards.

### Market structure and competition

The pharmaceutical industry can be divided into two segments. A small number of multinational companies conduct pharmaceutical research and development and own significant patent portfolios. They include Bayer, Boehringer Ingelheim, Bristol-Myers Squibb, GlaxoSmithKline, Merck, Pfizer, and Schering-Plough. Some of these originator companies own the patents for the ARVs now on the market. There are also a large number of generic suppliers, which compete in markets for off-patent drugs. Such markets exist where patents have expired or in countries where patents were never sought (perhaps because patent protection was unavailable). Generic manufacturers can be found in a large number of developing countries. Major producer nations include Brazil, China, India, and Thailand.

The market competition for a drug depends on its patent status. For on-patent drugs, the market structure is best seen as monopolistic for a therapeutic group. The pricing power of the patent monopoly depends on the availability and price of substitutes. Close and cheap substitutes may limit the ability of research-based pharmaceutical companies to set prices substantially above their variable production costs—though much depends on market demand. In addition to patent protection, pharmaceutical companies can generate pricing power by actively marketing their products to doctors and patients, creating brand loyalty. This pricing power is more relevant for retail markets—it typically is less important in public procurement.

For off-patent drugs, competition among generic producers can drive prices toward production costs. The price-reducing effect of generic competition can be observed when patents expire and generic producers are allowed to enter the market. But markets still may not be perfectly competitive. For example, the drugs sold by the original patent holders sometimes continue to be sold at a price premium in retail markets after patents have expired, due to brand loyalty. Governments can limit the scope for such post-patent price premiums by imposing generic substitution policies that force doctors to prescribe cheaper versions of pharmaceutically equivalent products.

Since patents are granted on a national basis, the patent status depends on the country in question (see chapter 2, "Intellectual Property Rights"). So, the type of competition for the supply of ARVs can vary significantly from country to country.

### Demand for drugs

Where drugs are sold in competitive markets and prices are driven toward production costs, demand-side influences have no bearing on drug prices. But when pharmaceutical companies have pricing power—say, due to patent protection—demand-side characteristics are important in determining a company's pricing decisions.

Demand characteristics depend on whether drugs are sold in retail markets or public procurement markets. In retail markets, the selection, payment, and consumption of drugs may involve up to four different parties: doctor, insurer, pharmacist, and patient. The influence of each party on demand depends on institutional attributes, including prescription policies, the coverage of health insurance, and the content of health insurance plans. As a rough rule, the smaller the coverage of health insurance and the lower the income of patients, the more that demand will be sensitive to prices, leading companies to fix lower prices. But if there is a small share of rich patients with health insurance, companies may set prices significantly above costs—especially if low-income patients could not afford drugs even if priced at cost. This may be a realistic description of pharmaceutical demand in many developing countries.

In public procurement markets, the price of off-patent drugs is generally determined through competitive bidding among suppliers. When drugs are protected by exclusive patent rights (and no flexibilities are available under TRIPS—see Annex B), the only method of procurement available in the absence of a compulsory license is direct contracting (also referred to as single sourcing). In this case, the public purchaser's ability to obtain lower prices depends on the size of the procurement contract. As will be further discussed in the next section, pooled procurement arrangements can enhance the bargaining power of the public purchaser and reduce prices.

### *Market segmentation, differential pricing, and equity pricing*

When pharmaceutical producers have pricing power, it is most profitable for them to fix different prices in different markets, according to market-specific demand characteristics. Such price differentiation can occur between countries and within countries, as when a manufacturer offers different prices to wholesalers and public purchasers.

For price differentiation to be sustainable, markets have to be segmented. If arbitrageurs or parallel traders are permitted to buy drugs in low-price markets and resell them in high-price markets, a uniform pricing structure across markets is likely to emerge. Producers can to some extent prevent parallel trade between markets by inserting clauses in purchasing contracts, proscribing the reselling of drugs by the purchaser or any third party. In addition, governments can outlaw the parallel import of drugs sold in foreign markets by adopting a rule of national intellectual property exhaustion. For a more detailed discussion of the exhaustion rule, see Annex B.

A concept related to price differentiation strategies is equity pricing. The general idea is to have the poor pay less than the rich, to make drugs affordable to patients of all income classes. Equity pricing may not always conflict with profit-oriented price differentiation strategies. As discussed previously, low-income patients are likely to be more price-sensitive, leading companies to fix lower prices.[50] In addition, philanthropic considera-

---

[50] A pricing concept that is sometimes mentioned in this context is the Ramsey pricing model, developed to efficiently regulate the prices of public utilities that need to recover fixed infrastructure costs. Some academic economists have applied this concept to economically efficient pharmaceutical pricing when patent holders need to recover sunk research and development investments. But other economists are skeptical whether actual pharmaceutical prices fit the Ramsey pricing model.

tions can induce companies to offer lower prices to poor countries or consumers. Shareholders in the research-based pharmaceutical industry expect companies to be good citizens. Failure to meet this expectation leads to public criticism from NGOs and the media, a damaged reputation, and a deterioration of customer relations and business climate in developed country markets.

Such an outcome is not guaranteed. First, even if prices are cheaper in low-income markets, they may still be substantially above production costs. For a drug protected by a patent, this cost may be difficult to determine, unless one has competitive benchmark prices from countries where the same drug is off patent. Second, even though parallel imports are generally prohibited in developed country markets, pharmaceutical companies may opt for uniform high pricing to preempt the illegal smuggling of drugs from low-price to high-price markets. A related concern is that pharmaceutical companies may in some markets face price controls that are based on prices of the same drugs in foreign markets. Setting uniform prices across countries may avoid the incidence of low price references.

Are equity pricing structures observed in practice? In a nutshell, it seems that multinational companies that own the drug patents offer steep price discounts to developing country governments, international purchase funds, and not-for-profit organizations—sometimes even undercutting the prices offered by generic producers. But wholesale prices do not appear to be systematically cheaper in low-income markets. A variety of factors are likely to account for this different pricing behavior. As already discussed, governments have bargaining power and can bargain for lower prices. Public pressure to lower prices may also be greater in government markets, where prices are typically more transparent. And the risk of legal and illegal parallel trade is substantially lower when drugs are sold to the public sector. Health authorities have a greater interest that the purchased drugs reach the patients in need than drug wholesalers, who are not directly responsible to patients.

## Additional price determinants in retail markets

Although the focus of this chapter is on public procurement, it is helpful to briefly mention additional determinants of prices that apply mostly to pharmaceutical wholesale and retail prices. First, many governments throughout the developed and developing world control pharmaceutical prices to contain medical expenditures, with pricing regulations differing from country to country. Price controls may apply at the wholesale or retail level. They may be based on estimates of production costs, on prices of therapeutically similar drugs on the market, or on an average of prices in foreign markets (reference pricing).

Second, the organization and efficiency of drug distribution determines the difference between the final retail price and the manufacturer selling price. If distribution markets are concentrated or even monopolized, wholesalers and retailers may be able to add large profit margins to prices. In some developing countries, drug distributors are state-owned companies, perhaps providing services less efficiently than a private supplier.

Third, various forms of taxation may push up prices, with value-added and sales taxes most relevant, along with import tariffs when drugs are purchased from foreign producers.[51]

## How can public purchasers bargain for low prices?

This section elaborates on the key strategies public purchasers can pursue to bargain for low prices. The discussion focuses on public procurement and does not address strategies for restraining retail prices for HIV/AIDS drugs.

The public procurement process and the main areas of government action depend on a drug's supply structure (figure 6.2). The method of procurement depends critically on the patent status of the selected drug. For off-patent drugs, multiple sourcing is possible, and prices can be determined through competitive bidding. The same holds for on-patent drugs for which voluntary or compulsory licenses have been issued. For other on patent drugs, only single-sourcing is possible and prices depend on the offers of the patent-holding company.

The protection of patents entails a tradeoff between incentives for research and development and the competitive provision of pharmaceutical products. Each country has to define its public health priorities and decide which side of the tradeoff should receive greater emphasis.

---

[51] According to a study by the WHO and WTO (2002), average import tariffs on final pharmaceutical products and active pharmaceutical ingredients are generally low or moderate in the developing world, although a number of exceptions exist.

**Figure 6.2  Drug procurement and options for lowering prices**

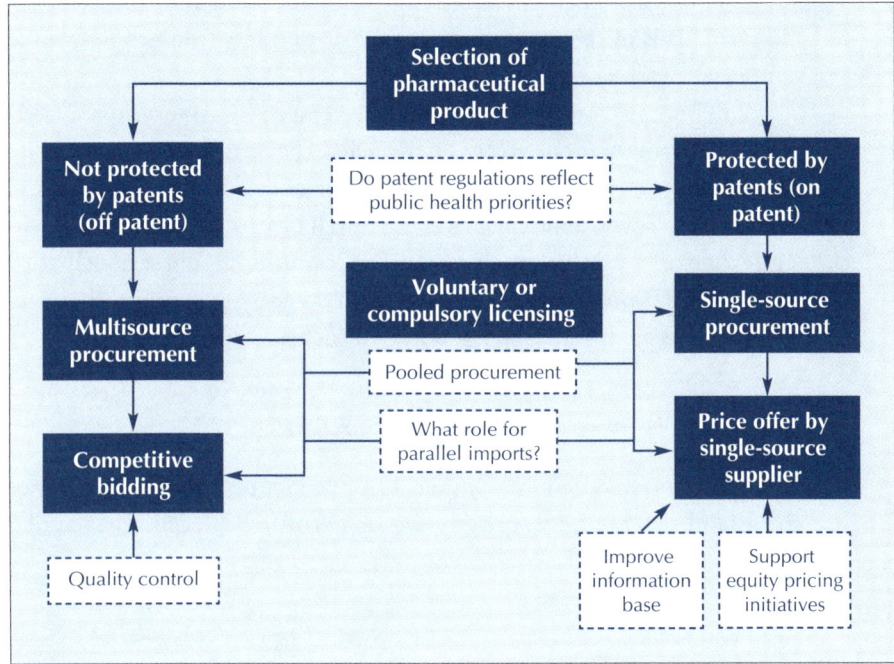

Important variables that determine these priorities include the share of the population infected with HIV, the social and economic consequences of the HIV/AIDS epidemic, and the financial resources available to combat the disease.

In the formulation of patent legislation and regulations, it is important that public procurement agencies and health ministries work together with other government agencies responsible for intellectual property policy (including ministries of commerce, trade, and industry). Otherwise, emerging patent rules may not take public health priorities sufficiently into account.

### Pooled procurement arrangements

Pooled procurement arrangements can promote lower prices in both multisource and single-source procurement settings. By increasing the purchase volume under the procurement contract, suppliers can reap economies of scale and lower their operational costs. In addition, pooled procurement arrangements strengthen the bargaining power of the purchaser. This is of special importance for price offers from single-source suppliers.

Pooling can take place at various levels (box 6.1). For example, a centralized procurement program by the federal government can substitute for procurement by states or even smaller entities (hospitals). At the international level, donor agencies can purchase drugs for distribution in more than one country. Small developing countries should seriously consider regional procurement arrangements—notwithstanding the legal complexities and political sensitivities of such arrangements.

### What role is there for parallel imported drugs?

It is sometimes argued that parallel imports can be a source of cheaper drugs and that such imports should be permitted. Recall that parallel

---

**Box 6.1 Examples of pooled procurement initiatives**

In Thailand, government hospitals—after the decentralization of health services—formed group-purchasing cooperatives. With a centralized procurement system, they were able to bring prices down as well as assure quality across the board by limiting themselves to certified suppliers. Individual hospitals managed their own supplier payments, drug stocks, inventory, and reordering, thus maintaining the benefits of decentralization.[52]

The Eastern Caribbean Drug Service was established in 1986 to manage the procurement process of the combined needs of eastern Caribbean states. Previously, individual countries managed their own procurement, at varying prices (in one instance, up to 30% higher than what was being paid elsewhere in the region). The service established a system for pooling needs, selectively and competitively accepting bids from suppliers, guaranteeing payment, monitoring supply, and assuring quality. In the first year of operation, countries of the eastern Caribbean saw (on average) a 44% price reduction in the cost of their pharmaceuticals.[53]

---

[52] Managing Drug Supply: Management Sciences for Health, in collaboration with WHO, Kumarian Press, 1997.
[53] Ibid.

imports are imports of drugs that have already been put on the market in a foreign country. In principle, such opportunities may well arise for single-source drugs, for which larger international price differentials are more likely to emerge.

For public procurement authorities three factors should caution against strong reliance on parallel imports:

- First, the sources of parallel imports are most likely limited to foreign retail markets. Drugs sold to public health authorities are typically protected against resale through contractual obligations, and indeed, public health authorities have an interest that the drugs reach the patients in need. Available evidence suggests that drugs are typically more expensive in retail markets, so parallel imports may offer no savings.[54]
- Second, governments should take into account the effect that parallel imports have on a foreign market. Pharmaceutical companies may respond by raising prices or curtailing supply to the foreign market, hurting patients in need in that country.
- Third, parallel imports are not directly sold by the drug producer, but by a wholesaler or other middleman. While there is no presumption that parallel imports are subquality products, the control of drug quality may become more complicated and require adequate regulatory capacity.

### Better information

Procurement agencies can enhance their bargaining power by collecting available information on production costs and prices. This is especially important for prices offered by single-source suppliers, for which no "invisible hand" in the form of competition exists. International price comparisons can provide useful benchmarks of the lowest prices available worldwide. As noted earlier, price comparisons should be based on prices at similar points in the supply chain. But where directly comparable price

---

[54] In addition, cheaper prices in foreign retail markets are often due to short-term exchange rate movements, limiting the sustainability of cheaper foreign supplies from one particular source in the longer term.

data are not available, rules of thumb—for example, using reasonable assumptions for transport costs, taxes, and wholesaler margins—may offer price estimates to derive realistic price floors. Larger agencies may have greater capacity to collect available pricing data, again favoring pooled procurement arrangements (box 6.2).

### Equity pricing initiatives

For single-source procurement, international equity pricing structures can be a way of offering lower prices to poorer nations. To a large extent, equity pricing relies on the unilateral decisions of pharmaceutical companies. But government initiatives can provide incentives that favor price discounts for countries less well off. Developed countries can offer a clear commitment to enforce regulations against unlawful parallel imports as well as restraint in using low-price references in rich country pharmaceutical price regulations (box 6.3). Developing countries can support equity pricing structures by allowing for contractual obligations to prevent the resale of publicly procured drugs—along with a commitment to enforce these obligations as permitted by the capacity of the public distribution system.

---

### Box 6.2 Sources of information on production costs and prices

**World Health Organization**
Drug Price Information Service: www.who.int/medicines/organization/par/ipc/drugpriceinfo.shtml

**Médicins Sans Frontières**
Information on prices and special discounts available to developing countries is available at: www.accessmed-msf.org/index.asp
   This website also publishes the document "Untangling the Web of Price Reductions—A Pricing Guide for the Purchase of ARVs for Developing Countries," which is updated regularly.

**UNICEF Supply Division**
Publication "Sources and Prices of Selected Drugs and Diagnostics for People Living with HIV/AIDS." www.unicef.org/supply/sources_and_prices_aids_report.pdf

### Box 6.3 Evidence of equity pricing for ARVs

Despite the considerable policy debate about equity pricing, empirical evidence on actual international pricing patterns by research-based pharmaceutical companies is surprisingly scant. One study has analyzed the wholesale prices of 15 AIDS drugs in 18 low- and middle-income nations, over the years 1995 to 1999.[55] It finds only a "faint indication of a systematic income-correlated [pricing] pattern."

By contrast, the pricing guide published by Médicins Sans Frontières details price discounts for ARVs offered by pharmaceutical companies to governments, NGOs, and certain international organizations distributing drugs in the developing world.[56] These prices are typically significantly cheaper than published retail prices in rich country markets. Keep in mind that most antiretrovirals are still unprotected by patents in many developing countries, and the lower prices may be partly due to competitive pressure from generic producers.

### European Union initiative on equity pricing

In May 2003, European governments adopted a regulation that promotes the cheap supply of medicines to combat HIV/AIDS, malaria, and tuberculosis to developing countries—by providing the legal framework to ensure that drugs are not diverted back to the European Union.[57]

Pharmaceutical manufacturers are invited to put their products on a tiered-price list, run by the European Commission. To be added to the list, medicines have to be available either at a price 75% below the average ex factory price in OECD countries or at the cost of production plus 15%. The products on the list are to bear a logo allowing customs to easily identify them. Being on this list and bearing the logo will mean that imports of these products into the EU for free circulation, re-exportation, warehousing, or transshipment are prohibited. Re-importation into the EU is prohibited from 76 countries, including least developed countries, low-income countries, and those where HIV/AIDS is particularly prevalent.

---

[55] See F. M. Scherer and J. Watal. 2002. "Post-TRIPS Options for Access to Patented Medicines in Developing Nations," *Journal of International Economic Law*, pp. 913–39.

[56] See "Untangling the Web of Price Reductions—A Pricing Guide for the Purchase of ARVs for Developing Countries," regularly updated edition, Médecins Sans Frontières, (www. accessmed-msf.org/index.asp)

[57] See europa.eu.int/comm/trade/csc/med08_en.htm.

# Estimating Resource Requirements for AIDS Treatment

## Case study: Estimating resource requirements for AIDS treatment in Burkina Faso

A recent World Bank supervision mission to Burkina Faso provided technical support to government counterparts in launching an ART project. The mission was expected to review and agree on a set of priority interventions to be funded during 2002, taking into account activities of other key development partners; review implementation and institutional arrangements; and initiate work on the ART to respond to the government's request for International Development Association assistance in this area.[1]

In 2003 Burkina Faso's HIV prevalence rate was 4 percent.[2] The key decision facing the government was whether, in what form, how, and when to embark on ART for people affected with HIV/AIDS.

---

[1] This case write-up is based on the mission report. But some data and results have been adjusted or further elaborated in order to better fit the purposes of this Guide.

[2] "Prevalence" measures the percentage of the population in question estimated to be affected. Schneidman, Miriam. 2002. *The Health System and the Poor: Draft Report on Burkina Faso.* World Bank, Washington, D.C.

### Relevant data and information

To make an acceptably accurate assessment of an ART program in Burkina Faso, at least the following information should be available. Otherwise, the best available estimates must be used:

- GDP of the country
- Amount of government spending on health care
- Budget shares for government spending in all sectors, including health
- Prevalence of HIV
- Current acquisition price of ARVs
- Potentially available best prices of ARVs in the world market
- Amount of donor funds available to the country to implement ART
- Current allocation of funds within HIV/AIDS issues, especially on prevention
- Currently prevailing health and development challenges facing the country
- Documented experiences of ART in Burkina Faso, if any.

**Key statistics within Burkina Faso in 2003 were:**

- Average household spending for health: $8 (rural $4, urban $21)
- Share of total household health spending going to medicines: 83 percent (rural 89 percent, urban 78 percent)
- Public health spending as a share of GDP, 2001: 2.1 percent
- Public health spending as a share of government spending, 2003: 9.8 percent
- Total expenditure on health, 2003: 4 percent of GDP

### Analysis

Projections of the evolution of the HIV/AIDS epidemic (based on the most recent available data) under alternative assumptions resulted in different future scenarios.[3] Assuming a 4 percent HIV prevalence in 2005, the consultant calculated the most conservative of these scenarios.

---

[3] Neither the information nor the time available for the study allowed for considering the long-term consequences, or for directly assessing existing health capacity to treat HIV/AIDS.

To account for the impact of a hypothetical ARV program on the survival of people living with AIDS, the consultant assumed that the number of people with AIDS under the 4 percent scenario would increase in 2005 from 33,245 (report estimation) to 35,723 and in 2010 from 40,000 to 54,646 (table A.1).

## Cost of ARVs

The average price negotiated by the Purchasing Agency of Generic Essential Medicines and Medical Supplies (CAMEG) of an ARV combination available to Burkina Faso was $1,000 (per person per year). In a proposal to the Global Fund to Fight AIDS, Tuberculosis and Malaria, it was estimated that ARVs would cost $1,410. At the same time, ARVs were available from Cipla (a low-cost generic manufacturer) for about $333 per person per year and from the Clinton Foundation's initiative on HIV/AIDS at a further discounted price of $140 per person per year[4] (table A.2).

Under the more optimistic assumptions, the projected cost of ART for all people with AIDS in Burkina Faso would be 0.14% of GDP and

### Table A.1  People living with HIV/AIDS in Burkina Faso, 2003–10

| Group | 2003 | 2005[a] | 2010 |
|---|---|---|---|
| Population with HIV/AIDS | 270,000 | 305,0000 | 365,000 |
| Population with AIDS | 29,500 | 33,245 | 40,000 |
| Population with AIDS (receiving ART) | 29,500 | 35,723 | 54,646 |

a. Estimated assuming an 4% baseline prevalence of HIV in 2005.
*Source:* Estimates from World Bank mission report.

---

[4] Quoted in, among other sources, "Clinton Program Would Help Poor Nations Get AIDS Drugs"—*Wall Street Journal*—October 23, 2003.

**Table A.2  Projected cost of ART (drugs only) for all people with AIDS under high cost ($1000), low cost ($333), and lowest cost ($140) price scenarios, 2003–10**
(millions of U.S. dollars unless otherwise specified)

| Price scenario | 2003 | 2005 | 2010 |
| --- | --- | --- | --- |
| **At the CAMEG negotiated price ($1,000)** | **29.5** | **35.7** | **54.6** |
| –As share of GDP | 0.98 | 1.07 | 1.26 |
| –As share of health budget | 42.9 | 46.7 | 54.9 |
| **At Cipla's price offer to Médicins Sans Frontières ($333)** | **9.8** | **11.9** | **18.2** |
| –As share of GDP | 0.33 | 0.36 | 0.42 |
| –As share of health budget | 14.3 | 15.6 | 18.3 |
| **At Clinton Foundation price ($140)** | **4.1** | **5.0** | **7.7** |
| –As share of GDP | 0.14 | 0.15 | 0.18 |
| –As share of health budget | 6.0 | 6.5 | 7.7 |
| **GDP projections[a]** | **2,847** | **3,334** | **4,336** |
| Health budget projections | 65.3 | 76.5 | 99.5 |

a. Projections assume an annual real growth of 5.4% in 2003 and thereafter.
*Sources:* World Bank mission report, Budget Projections: IDA Program Document for a PPRS Credit to Burkina Faso, April 15, 2002, p.8, table 1; Sources and prices of selected medicines and diagnostics for people living with HIV/AIDS, A joint UNICEF—UNAIDS—WHO—MSF Project, June 2003 and Clinton Program Would Help Poor Nations Get AIDS Drugs, *Wall Street Journal*, October 23, 2003

6.0 percent of the health budget in 2003. The pessimistic case projects 0.98 percent of GDP and 42.9 percent of the health budget. These percentages would likely increase in the medium-term because ART increases survival and, hence, the prevalence of AIDS.

## Other costs

The main health care costs in ART, other than the cost of ARVs themselves, are associated with: non-ARVs, diagnostic tests, personnel, and equipment (table A.3).

**Table A.3  Projected total cost of ART, per person per year, 2003**
(U.S. dollars)

| Cost category | Lowest-cost scenario | High-cost scenario |
|---|---|---|
| ARV drugs | 140 | 1,000 |
| Other drugs | 80 | 80 |
| Biological monitoring | 150 | 400 |
| Personnel | 200 | 200 |
| Equipment | 50 | 50 |
| Total cost | 620 | 1,730 |

In 1999 Burkina Faso's health budget was $57.2 million, with 40 per-cent funded from external sources. Providing treatment to all people with AIDS would imply a significant increase in budget for 2005 (table A.4).

## Implications of the cost scenarios

The price of ARV drugs is a major variable in the total cost of an ARV program. Depending on the country, other associated costs (such as

**Table A.4  Projected total cost of ART for all people with AIDS in Burkina Faso, under high cost ($1,730), and lowest cost ($620) price scenarios, 2003–10**
(millions of U.S. dollars)

| | 2003 | 2005 | 2010 |
|---|---|---|---|
| High-cost scenario | 51.0 | 61.8 | 94.5 |
| Lowest-cost scenario | 18.3 | 22.1 | 33.9 |

Source: Estimates from World Bank mission report.

personnel) also contribute significantly to total cost. Up to 2,000 patients might be cared for within the existing infrastructure in Burkina Faso. Significantly increasing that figure would probably require important investments in physical capacity and human resources. It is essential that the country procurement agency—the CAMEG—is able to take advantage of market conditions.

With an annual budget of $2 million it would be possible to provide ARVs for 2,000 to 14,285 patients, depending on the unit cost of the treatment obtained. If the full cost of treatment were covered, the number of patients treated would range between 1,156 and 3,225 in high and low cost scenarios.

Given the government's financial constraints, one possibility is introducing user fees (that is, having patients pay for all or part of their treatment). But this may radically affect the selection of patients, broadening the health divide and highlighting privileges and class differences among people living with HIV/AIDS.

Likely problems from small ART programs include:

- *Pressure to be selected.* Poorer people likely to be discriminated against.
- *Significant stress on health staff* from having to apply eligibility criteria.
- *Potential sharing of medication* among family members if not all those with the disease are selected for treatment.
- *A black market.* Even in the optimistic case that 14,285 patients (48 percent of people living with AIDS) are treated, a strong unsatisfied need, fueled by the likely political publicity of the program, could increase demand from relatively affluent people. People with low incomes might have an incentive to divert part of the $1,000 worth of medication to the market, especially if there are adverse effects in the course of treatment. Noncompliance, the loss of effectiveness, and the appearance of resistance could also result.

## Complicating the resource estimation model and applying it to other contexts

Program implementation requires investments in physical and human capital that cannot be estimated simply by multiplying patients treated and average cost. For large increases in the number of patients treated, it is essential to assess the used and unused health system capacity and the additional investments in physical and human capital required for attaining specific coverage targets.

Introducing ART implies possible changes in the lifelong profile of treatment costs, an additional complication. The likely short-term effect of introducing or scaling up ART is an immediate increase in the health expenditures of the HIV/AIDS program. In the long term, the ART may reduce the rate of opportunistic infections and their associated costs, especially hospitalization. But improving ART allows people with HIV to live longer. So the life cycle costs for a single patient and the total spending on AIDS treatment are likely to grow if individual patterns and costs of care are maintained for an initial cohort of patients. The net impact on the costs of an individual's treatment, or on the total expenditure of an HIV/AIDS program, is thus uncertain and difficult to assess.

The parameters that define the epidemic and the required costs of treatment are likely to change. Simple statistical extrapolation of past data might be highly misleading, especially if the model aims at a distant time horizon. In any case, estimated numbers of people living with HIV/AIDS provided by statistical or epidemiological methods usually represent the maximum number of people to be treated, because only a proportion of the estimated number of people living with HIV/AIDS are likely to seek and obtain care. That proportion can also be extrapolated from past data, but it may change with ART programs. Experience from other countries where such change has already occurred might prove useful in assessing the likely effects.

Estimating the future evolution of an epidemic—and its associated costs—is highly speculative, due to the lack of information and the inherent uncertainty of the cost and effectiveness of available and future treatments. Transparency in the analytical procedures and assumptions for making projections will allow these projections to be easily adjusted as the parameters of the epidemic change, new treatments are introduced, or new evidence becomes available.

A simple model of financial resource estimation for an ART program would take at least the following factors into account:

- HIV prevalence rate and projections for the near future.
- GDP per capita and economic outlook for the country.

- Cost of ARVs (at current and best world prices, if different).
- International and national aid funding available for an ART program.

In addition to the factors detailed in the simple model, a complex model of resource estimation would take into consideration at least (and not conclusively) the following:

- Health infrastructure capacity (physical and human).
- Cost assumptions for scaling-up capacity to meet increased need.
- Different predictive assumptions of the impact of behavioral change.
- Different scenarios of new HIV incidence.
- An estimate of financial outflows and inflows (hospital care, productivity).
- Changes in household economic situations and the ability to pay for treatment.

Applying a simple model of resource requirements estimation to Kenya and South Africa, estimates of government spending and health sector budget outlays required for treating HIV/AIDS with ARVs, under different cost assumptions (tables A.5–A.8), are as follows:[5]

---

[5] This illustration for Kenya and South Africa estimates the growth in the HIV/AIDS epidemic and the growth rate in the number of people with clinical AIDS along the same assumptions as those used for Burkina Faso. In reality, it is likely that the rate of growth of HIV incidence differs across countries, due to a host of complex socioeconomic and political factors.

**Table A.5  Projected number of people living with HIV/AIDS in Kenya and South Africa, 2002–10**

|  | 2002 | 2005 | 2010 |
|---|---|---|---|
| **Kenya** | | | |
| Population with HIV/AIDS[a] | 2,500,000 | 2,825,000 | 3,390,000 |
| Population treated with ARVs (10%) | 250,000 | 282,500 | 339,000 |
| **South Africa** | | | |
| Population with HIV/AIDS[b] | 5,000,000 | 5,650,000 | 6,780,000 |
| Population treated with ARVs (10%) | 500,000 | 565,000 | 678,000 |

a. Data assume HIV/AIDS prevalence rate of ~8 percent, adult prevalence of ~15 percent.
b. Data assume HIV/AIDS prevalence rate of ~12 percent, adult prevalence of ~20 percent.
*Source:* www.unaids.org.

**Table A.6  Projected cost of ART (drugs only) for all people with AIDS in Kenya, under high cost ($1,000), low cost ($333), and lowest cost ($140) price scenarios, 2002–10**
(millions of U.S. dollars unless otherwise specified)

| Price scenario | 2002 | 2005 | 2010 |
|---|---|---|---|
| GDP projections[a] | 11,296 | 11,860 | 12,453 |
| Health budget projections[b] | 271.1 | 284.6 | 298.9 |
| ARV cost of $1,000 per person per year | 250 | 282.5 | 339 |
| –As share of GDP | 2.2 | 2.4 | 2.7 |
| –As share of health budget | 92.2 | 99.3 | 113.4 |
| ARV cost of $333 per person per year | 83.3 | 94.2 | 113 |
| –As share of GDP | 0.7 | 0.8 | 0.9 |
| –As share of health budget | 30.7 | 33.1 | 37.8 |
| ARV cost of $140 per person per year | 35.0 | 39.6 | 47.5 |
| –As share of GDP | 0.3 | 0.3 | 0.4 |
| –As share of health budget | 12.9 | 13.9 | 15.9 |

a. GDP projections are taken at 5 percent a year (consistent with Burkina Faso assumptions).
b. Health budget projections are held constant at 2002 (percentage of total GDP) terms.
*Source:* GDP projections from World Bank country GINA data, www.worldbank.org. Health budget data from UNDP *Human Development Report 2003,* www.undp.org/hdr2003/indicator/cty_f_KEN.html.

**Table A.7  Projected cost of ART (drugs only) for all people with AIDS in South Africa, under high cost ($1,000), low cost ($333), and lowest cost ($140) price scenarios, 2002–10**
(millions of U.S. dollars unless otherwise specified)

| Price scenario | 2002 | 2005 | 2010 |
|---|---|---|---|
| GDP projections[a] | 113,492 | 119,167 | 125,125 |
| Health budget projections[b] | 4,199 | 4,409 | 4,630 |
| ARV cost of $1,000 per person per year | 500 | 565 | 678 |
| –As share of GDP | 0.44 | 0.47 | 0.54 |
| –As share of health budget | 12 | 12.8 | 14.6 |
| ARV cost of $333 per person per year | 166.6 | 188.3 | 225.8 |
| –As share of GDP | 0.15 | 0.16 | 0.18 |
| –As share of health budget | 4.0 | 4.3 | 4.9 |
| ARV cost of $140 per person per year | 70.0 | 79.0 | 94.9 |
| –As share of GDP | 0.06 | 0.07 | 0.08 |
| –As share of health budget | 1.7 | 1.8 | 2.1 |

a. GDP projections are taken at 5 percent a year (consistent with Burkina Faso assumptions).
b. Health budget projections are held constant at 2002 (percentage of total GDP) terms.
*Source:* GDP projections from World Bank country GINA data, www.worldbank.org. Health budget data from UNDP Human Development Report 2003, www.undp.org/hdr2003/indicator/cty_f_ZAF.html.

### Table A.8  Projected total costs of ART, per person per year, in Kenya and South Africa
(U.S. dollars)

| Cost category | Lowest-cost scenario | | High-cost scenario | |
|---|---|---|---|---|
| | Kenya | South Africa | Kenya | South Africa |
| ARVs | 140 | 140 | 1,000 | 1,000 |
| Other drugs | 80 | 80 | 80 | 80 |
| Biological monitoring | 150 | 150 | 400 | 400 |
| Personnel[a] | 200 | 1,020 | 200 | 1,020 |
| Equipment | 50 | 50 | 50 | 50 |
| Total | 620 | 1,440 | 1,730 | 2,550 |

a. For illustrative purposes, we assume similar wage structures in Kenya and Burkina Faso. Wage structures in South Africa were estimated using figures reported in UNDP's *Human Development Report 2003*. The average GDP per capita for the poorest 80 percent of South Africans is compared with the average GDP per capita for all of Kenya to find an illustrative wage multiplier (the figure used here is 5.1).
*Source:* Author calculations based on UNDP *Human Development Report 2003*.

# B

## *Intellectual Property Rights: How They Affect Procurement and What Steps Can Be Taken*

Intellectual property rights affect all kinds of commodities, but they are especially important for HIV/AIDS medicines and related goods. Intellectual property rights influence:

- The availability of goods in a country.
- The opportunities for importing goods from another country.
- The competition between equivalent goods from different producers, specifically between products of originator (or innovator) companies and those of generic producers.
- Price competition and getting value-for-money in public health.

Many HIV/AIDS medicines and laboratory products are relatively new, still protected by patents granted to the originators, usually within countries where the originator has, or expects to have, a significant market. But the patent situation varies widely across countries, affected by such international agreements as the Agreement on Trade-Related Aspects of Intellectual Property Rights (TRIPS). That makes it important for staff responsible for project implementation to assimilate the information in this chapter. Early clarification of the intellectual property rights situation (and of registration requirements and import regulations) will prevent frustration, wasted time and money, and possible litigation. The chapter covers:

- Intellectual property rights—what are they?
- The TRIPS Agreement—the international regulatory situation of intellectual property rights.
- National regulatory situations and TRIPS-compliant flexibilities for least developed and developing WTO member countries.
- Determining the patent status of HIV/AIDS medicines in a particular country.
- The chapter ends with a brief consideration of the relevance of trade-marks and copyrights.

## Intellectual property rights—what are they?

Intellectual property rights include patents, trademarks, copyrights, and rights in data assembled for regulatory purposes (rights in data are not strictly "intellectual property"). HIV/AIDS medicines may be subject to claims based on any of these rights, which may affect medicine procurement in different ways.

A *patent* is granted to the inventor of a product or process and gives the inventor the right to exclude others from making, using, selling, offering for sale, and importing a product covered by a "product" patent,[1] and from using a process covered by a "process" patent.[2] Patents are granted on a country-to-country basis, and sometimes on a regional basis. The duration is typically 20 years from the filing of the patent application, but this term may vary. Because of cost and other factors (including differences in national legislative arrangements) associated with patenting, it is common for a particular medicine to be patented in some countries and not in others. This is the case for many HIV/AIDS medicines, including ARVs and medicines used to treat opportunistic infections, cancer, and other AIDS-related conditions. There are limitations on and exceptions to patent protection that benefit public procurement authorities.

---

[1] The right to prevent importation does not prevent "parallel importation" of a patented medicine when a rule of international exhaustion of patent rights is followed. This is discussed later.
[2] As well as to exclude others from using, selling, offering for sale, and importing a product produced by a patented process.

A *trademark* is a sign used to distinguish the products of one enterprise from those of other enterprises. A trademark gives its holder the right to prevent others from using it in commerce in a manner likely to confuse consumers. Most medicines are known by the trademark(s) of one or more producers (the exclusive commercial name), as well as by a scientific or generic name (such as the international nonproprietary name that can be used by anyone).[3] Like patents, trademarks are granted on a country-to-country (and regional) basis. The registered trademark applicable to the same medicine may differ from country to country.[4] Trademark protection is limited by important "fair use" rights that permit common references to trademarked medicines.

A *copyright* is granted to the author of an expressive work (such as a book or design) and gives its holder the right to exclude others from reproducing or distributing the copyrighted work. Copyright protection does not extend to information (such as historical data and records) or to ideas (such as scientific content).[5] Although copyright is not commonly associated with medicines, it is sometimes claimed (and sometimes misused) by producers to preclude the duplication or distribution of the packaging or information materials accompanying a medicine (such as doctor and patient leaflets).

*Rights in data* may be asserted on the basis of national (or regional) legislation covering information submitted to drug regulatory authorities, such as the authority that approves the safety, efficacy, quality, or bioequivalence of a medicine in the registration process. Rights in data

---

[3] A list of international nonproprietary names for pharmaceutical substances (such as amoxicillin, ampicillin, nandrolone, temazepam, phenobarbital, amphetamine, ibuprofen, chloroquine, and retinol) is maintained by the WHO. WHO members are expected to refrain from granting trademark status to international nonproprietary names.

[4] Medicines are sometimes referred to as "branded" or "brand name" medicines. Sometimes that means the same thing as "trademarked" medicine. At other times, "branded" or "brand name" is used to refer in a more general way to the company that makes the medicine, for example, a "Glaxo"-brand or "Pfizer"-brand product. A major producer might market the same medicine under a number of different trademarks (or specific names), but all those medicines would be "branded" medicines of the company that produces them. From a legal standpoint, the concept of "branded" or "brand name" in the sense of the company (or "trade name") is not usually the basis for a formal legal action. Such actions, rather, are brought on the basis of the specific "trademark" for the medicine that is registered within a particular country.

[5] Copyright law distinguishes between expression and information (such as historical data or scientific content). Some countries have adopted unique "database" protection laws to address what they consider a gap in protection. Other countries have rejected this approach.

protect against the "unfair commercial use" of certain information contained in regulatory submissions. Rights in data are limited by public interest considerations. Public noncommercial use of data generally does not interfere with such rights.

## The TRIPS Agreement—the international regulatory situation of intellectual property rights

On January 1, 1995, the WTO was established as successor to the General Agreement on Tariffs and Trade (GATT). The WTO includes agreements regulating trade in goods and services. The most important from the standpoint of medicines procurement is the TRIPS Agreement, which obligates the nearly 150 members of the WTO to effect certain rules on the protection of intellectual property rights.

To take account of the different economic and social circumstances of WTO members, the TRIPS Agreement includes various "transitional" arrangements that directly affect patents on medicines and other intellectual property rights. In addition—as a consequence of the WTO Ministerial Declaration on the TRIPS Agreement and Public Health, adopted in Doha on November 14, 2001—transitional arrangements in favor of "least developed" WTO members were extended in important ways.

TRIPS Agreement rules affecting medicines, including those for treatment of HIV/AIDS, have been the subject of substantial and sometimes heated controversy between WTO members. To a large extent, this has reflected a difference between developed and developing members in their perceptions of the costs and benefits of protecting patents in medicines.

The idea behind granting patents is that by providing a potential financial reward to the inventor of a new product, such as a medicine, innovation and investment are encouraged to the benefit of the public. A new medicine may be costly (and risky) to develop, but easy to reverse-engineer and copy. Patents provide a means to allow innovators to recover their investments and to make profits that could be used to further develop new medicines.

The TRIPS Agreement takes into account the potential social cost of medicines patents in a variety of ways, acknowledging and allowing certain flexibilities. Despite the inclusion of these flexibilities in the TRIPS

Agreement, developing country WTO members were concerned with pressures being exerted on them to rigidly apply a fixed set of patent rules. They demanded that WTO Ministers expressly acknowledge and affirm their right to flexibly implement TRIPS obligations.

In the Doha Declaration on the TRIPS Agreement and Public Health,[6] WTO Ministers:

- Agreed that the TRIPS Agreement "does not and should not prevent Members from taking measures to protect public health" and "that the Agreement can and should be interpreted and implemented in a manner supportive of WTO Members' right to protect public health and, in particular, to promote access to medicines for all."[7]
- Recognized that each WTO member is permitted to adopt its own regime for the "exhaustion of intellectual property rights without challenge."[8] This means that members are free to permit "parallel importation" of medicines.
- Recognized that "Each Member has the right to grant compulsory licenses and the freedom to determine the grounds upon which such licenses are granted."[9]
- In connection with a rule that permits the granting of compulsory licenses without prior negotiations with the patent holder when there is a national emergency, other circumstances of extreme urgency or for public noncommercial use, recognized that "Each Member has the right to determine what constitutes a national emergency or other circumstances of extreme urgency, it being understood that public health crises, including those relating to HIV/AIDS, tuberculosis, malaria and other epidemics, can represent a national emergency or other circumstances of extreme urgency."[10]

The Doha Declaration, in its paragraph 6, made provision for further negotiations on the effective use of compulsory licensing by members with insufficient or no manufacturing capacity. The results of these negotiations will be discussed later.

---

[6–10] WTO Ministerial Conference, Declaration on the TRIPS Agreement and Public Health, adopted November 14, 2001, Fourth Session, Doha, WT/MIN(01)/DEC/2 (November 20, 2001).

WTO Ministers agreed in paragraph 7 of the Doha Declaration that least developed members should not be obligated to implement or apply TRIPS provisions for pharmaceutical product patents or data protection until January 1, 2016. Just as important, they agreed that least developed members already allowing for such protection did not need to "enforce" such rules until that later date.[11] The TRIPS Council adopted a decision confirming this flexibility.[12] And the WTO General Council added a waiver of least developed members' obligations regarding so-called exclusive marketing rights that might otherwise have been used as a substitute for patent protection to block production, import, and sale of medicines.

To sum up this far:

- The WTO TRIPS Agreement establishes minimum standards of intellectual property rights protection. It also incorporates basic "flexibilities" that can be used to overcome intellectual property rights-related barriers to acquiring low-cost medicines.
- The Doha Declaration on the TRIPS Agreement and Public Health strongly affirmed the right of governments to promote and protect public health by taking advantage of the flexibilities in the TRIPS Agreement to provide access to medicines "for all." Special new rules were adopted in favor of least developed countries.
- "Least developed" countries are specially favored under new TRIPS Agreement rules. They have maximum flexibility to disregard patents and data protection rules until at least 2016.

## National regulatory situations and TRIPS-compliant flexibilities for different countries

Every nation has an inherent right to protect the health of its people. Intellectual property rules cannot take away this fundamental right.

---

[11] Providing in relevant part: "We also agree that the least-developed country Members will not be obliged, with respect to pharmaceutical products, to implement or apply Sections 5 and 7 of Part II of the TRIPS Agreement or to enforce rights provided for under these Sections until 1 January 2016, without prejudice to the right of least-developed country Members to seek other extensions of the transition periods as provided for in Article 66.1 of the TRIPS Agreement. We instruct the Council for TRIPS to take the necessary action to give effect to this pursuant to Article 66.1 of the TRIPS Agreement." (Declaration on the TRIPS Agreement and Public Health, para. 7).

[12] Decision of the Council for TRIPS of June 27, 2002 (www.wto.org/english/tratop_e/trips_e/public_health_e.htm)

To facilitate the low-cost acquisition of HIV/AIDS-related medicines and supplies, national laws and regulations generally should provide for the flexibilities permitted by the TRIPS Agreement. But even without pre-existing national legislation, the government always retains the power to act to protect the public interest. The TRIPS Agreement does not require that all necessary measures a government may take shall have been the subject of pre-existing legislation.

It is important in the formulation of national legislation and regulations that the various departments with responsibilities for importing and distributing medicines cooperate and coordinate their activities. It is all too common that the departments responsible for public health, trade, and intellectual property rights regulation do not communicate with each other in the development of their regulatory authority. As a result they may end up working with inconsistent rules.

The term "generic" is used in different ways for medicines.[13] Here it refers to originally patented medicines that are later produced off patent. If a generic medicine is lawfully available in an exporting country, a procurement authority in an importing country is concerned only with the patent situation in its own market.

Some HIV/AIDS-related medicines are not under patent in potential exporting countries. Why? Because patent protection for pharmaceutical products was made available only recently in those countries—or has not yet come into force. In some cases, the patent on a medicine will already have expired. In others, the medicine may be produced and marketed by a licensee under a government authorization that does not require the patent holder's consent.[14] Such generic (or off patent) medicines can be obtained in the exporting country without difficulty in the

---

[13] The term "generic" is also used more generally to refer to multisource products normally available from a wide range of manufacturers. Many drugstore retail chains, for example, sell their own generic brand of aspirin.

[14] Article 31(f) of the TRIPS Agreement provides that the predominant part of production under compulsory license shall be for supply of the domestic market of the country issuing the license. Medicine that would be available for export without additional measures would be the nonpredominant part of such production under compulsory license. On August 30, 2003, a new legal mechanism was adopted at the WTO that allows for the issuance of compulsory licenses for export at the request of eligible importing countries. This legal mechanism is discussed in note 27. Under this mechanism, additional measures are required in the exporting country.

sense that patents should not constitute an obstacle. Similarly, the producer of a generic medicine in an exporting country will typically use an identifier that either is an international nonproprietary name or that differs from the originator's brand name to avoid potential trademark infringement in its local market.

For medicines that are generic in the country of export, the potential intellectual property rights obstacles to procurement of HIV/AIDS-related medicines generally arise in the importing country, not the exporting country. (This assumes that there are generic medicines for purchase in an exporting country, and that is a question discussed later.)

If a medicine or supply is not protected by intellectual property rights (such as a patent) in the country of importation, intellectual property rights will not constitute an obstacle for the procurement authority.

The acquisition of HIV/AIDS-related medicines or supplies is complicated by the fact that intellectual property rights are generally granted for a particular country (or region). The presence or absence of a patent in one country does not ensure the presence or absence of a patent in another country. Even though a medicine, such as an ARV, may be off patent in India, it may not be in South Africa. Because of this, a patent holder in an importing country may object to the import of a medicine that has been lawfully produced and sold (is generic) in an exporting country, based on a patent in the importing country.

Whether the patent holder in the importing country will be able to block importation and distribution depends on various factors, including the legislation of the importing country, steps the government has taken or may take under that legislation, and the character of the purchase transaction. That is why it is important that governments pay attention to including TRIPS Agreement flexibilities in their national legal framework; that is, to allow for actions that are important to protecting public health.

### Least developed WTO member countries

Least developed countries are likely to face the greatest budgetary constraints in purchasing HIV/AIDS-related medicines and supplies. Several least developed countries have high rates of HIV-infection, and even with external financial support, it is extremely important that they obtain medicines at low prices.[15] Many ARVs are available from originators for least developed countries at special prices, and might be cheaper than generics. But if a government wants to buy generics, and if it is concerned that the originator(s) would enforce its patent(s), the following paragraphs explain how it may exercise its rights to buy generics. Some originators may voluntarily waive their enforcement rights.

Many least developed countries have legislation to grant patent protection, and almost all least developed countries have at least some legislation to grant trademark and copyright protection. Legislation in some least developed countries may provide for protection of data submitted for regulatory purposes.

The TRIPS Agreement took into account the special and differential interests of least developed WTO members in several ways, and the Ministerial Declaration on the TRIPS Agreement and Public Health accorded further special treatment for least developed countries. Least developed countries were initially allowed until January 1, 2006, to apply the provisions of the TRIPS Agreement (other than provisions relating to national and most favored nation treatment that applied to all members after one year) (Art. 66.1, TRIPS Agreement). While developing members were also allowed certain transitional exceptions from TRIPS obligations, these members were not permitted to reduce protection already in place during those transitional periods.[16] Least developed countries were not, however, subject to the prohibition against reducing existing levels of protection.[17] The allowance for least developed countries through January 1, 2006 applies to all forms of intellectual property rights.

As discussed earlier, decisions made by the TRIPS Council pursuant to paragraph 7 of the Declaration on the TRIPS Agreement and Public

---

[15] It is important that medicines are of assured quality. Procedures relating to quality assurance are discussed elsewhere in this Technical Guide. In this section, attention is only on intellectual property rights. There is no inherent correlation between intellectual property rights and quality in the sense that generic producers are capable of producing medicines of quality equal to that of intellectual property rights holders.

[16] Article 65.5 provides: "A Member availing itself of a transitional period under paragraphs 1, 2, 3 or 4 shall ensure that any changes in its laws, regulations and practice made during that period do not result in a lesser degree of consistency with the provisions of this Agreement."

[17] Article 66 defines the exception for least developed countries, and does not incorporate by reference or otherwise the prohibition against reducing levels of protection set out in Article 65.5. While there is a provision on the protection of existing subject matter in Article 70.2, that Article does not apply to least developed countries per the terms of Article 66.1.

Health allow least developed countries until January 1, 2016, to implement or enforce pharmaceutical product patent and data protection.

Under the TRIPS Agreement the effect of the various allowances in favor of least developed countries is that national authorities are free to reduce or eliminate protection for trademarks and copyrights at least until January 1, 2006.[18] And they may elect not to implement or enforce pharmaceutical product patent and data protection until at least January 1, 2016. All these actions are consistent with the TRIPS Agreement obligations of least developed countries.[19]

The fact that national decisions not to implement or to "disapply" intellectual property rights may be taken without violating TRIPS obligations still leaves it to the national authorities of each least developed country to take steps in the national legislative, administrative, or judicial framework.

While authority to disapply the above-mentioned TRIPS provisions does not need to be granted until the time it is exercised, and it may even be possible to grant it "after the fact," as in most legal matters, by acting in advance the government can save itself and its procurement authorities from the potential delay and expense involved in legal battles with intellectual property rights holders—and from potential political pressure from the home governments of intellectual property rights holders.

Because the political and constitutional arrangements in each country are somewhat different, it is difficult to offer general guidance on the specific steps least developed country governments should take to pave the way for avoiding intellectual property rights–based obstacles to procuring generic medicines and supplies. If the executive and parliament (or legislature) cooperate in adopting a grant of authority for the procurement authority to disapply intellectual property rights in order to promote and protect public health, this should in most or all least

---

[18] Consistent with their national treatment and most favored nation obligations under Articles 3–5, TRIPS Agreement.

[19] Least developed countries might initially appear to be acting inconsistently with the terms of the Paris or Berne Convention by, for example, interfering with a patent right, but Paris and Berne obligations outside the TRIPS context are not enforceable by trade sanctions. In any case, actions by governments in favor of least developed countries at the WTO should be understood to allow for the same exceptions to Paris and Berne Convention obligations under general principles of equity. Otherwise, the actions by the same governments at the WTO would be undertaken in manifest bad faith.

developed countries be adequate to accomplish the objective. Other procedures are certainly possible and acceptable.[20] The government should, however, avoid discriminating among intellectual property rights holders of different nationalities so as to comply with TRIPS Agreement national and most favored nation treatment requirements.

## Developing WTO member countries

The situation for developing member legislation and regulation is more complicated than that for least developed country authorities because of the applicability of TRIPS Agreement rules.

The procurement authority may choose to purchase locally or to import an ARV or other medicine directly from the patent holder or its authorized distributor. In such circumstances, intellectual property rights should not constitute an obstacle because the patent holder is expressly or by implication consenting to the sale and use of the medicine under its

### Box B.1  Parallel importing

*Exhaustion of rights.* When patented medicines are placed on the market in exporting countries B–E, the patent right is exhausted in importing country A. The procurement authority in country A is free to import from the lower-priced markets—exporting countries B and E.

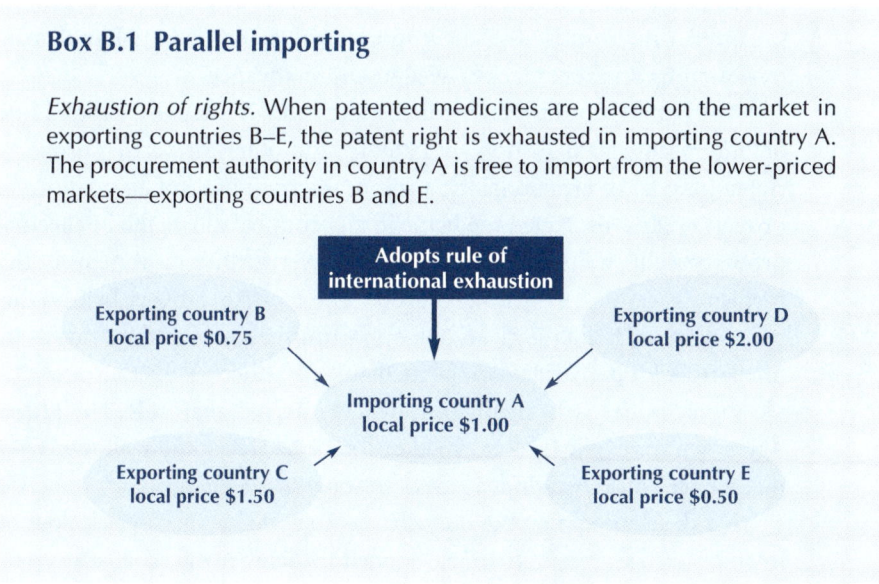

---

[20] Action by the executive or parliament alone may well be adequate (depending on the constitutional arrangement), and the courts might have authority to act on their own to disapply patent protection taking into account TRIPS Agreement principles.

patent. Even here, however, caution must be exercised. Recall that patents are granted and are independent for each country (or region). When a patent holder sells a medicine in one country, it gives up its right to further control the use or resale of the medicine in that country (the principle of "national exhaustion of rights"), including the right to resell the product for export. But if the patent holder holds a "parallel patent" in an importing member country, it might seek to block importation into that other country based on its locally held patent in that other country.

The procurement authority may find that it is purchasing medicines from a patent holder in an exporting country, rather than locally. If medicines are purchased from the holder of parallel patents in the exporting and importing member, the procurement authority should obtain an express promise from the seller (holder of the parallel patent) that it will not attempt to invoke its patent in the importing country. This promise may be in the form of the patent holder's acknowledgment that it is selling the medicines for import into the purchaser's country. A court in the importing country may decide that by selling the product for export the patent holder implicitly waived any right to invoke its parallel patent in the importing country. But the importer will avoid potential legal costs by obtaining an express acknowledgment in advance.

The country into which medicines are brought may also adopt a rule of "international exhaustion" of patents (and other intellectual property rights). Under international exhaustion, the lawful sale of an intellectual property rights–protected medicine in any country causes the intellectual property rights holder to give up control over further movement of the medicine regardless of national border. The economic theory behind this rule is that the holder is given one opportunity to exploit the value of its intellectual property rights in the medicine (or other product), not multiple opportunities as the medicine moves in international trade. The TRIPS Agreement, as explicitly confirmed by the Doha Declaration, allows WTO member countries to adopt a rule of international exhaustion.

If a developing member does so, the first sale by the patent holder or its authorized representative in an exporting member will exhaust any parallel intellectual property rights in the importing country[21]—and intellec-

---

[21] There is some debate about whether a medicine (or other product) sold under "compulsory license" (see definition below) in an exporting country will exhaust a patent in an importing

### Box B.2  Parallel imports in South Africa—under the rule of international exhaustion

South Africa has adopted legislation (Section 15C of the Medicines and Related Substances Control Amendment Act, No. 90 of 1997) pursuant to which its Minister of Health (through the Medicines Control Council) has issued regulations that establish the conditions for the parallel importation of medicines into the country. In addition to the regulations, the Council has issued a Guideline for Parallel Importation of Medicines in South Africa.

The regulations provide that: "parallel importation" means the importation into the Republic of a medicine protected under patent and/or registered in the Republic that has been put onto the market outside the Republic by or with the consent of such patent holder.

The regulations and guideline provide procedures under which a parallel importer must obtain a permit to undertake importation. These procedures are intended to ensure that parallel import medicines are duly approved and registered by the Department of Health, and that the parallel importer will comply with requirements ordinarily imposed on vendors of medicine in South Africa, such as using an approved storage facility and having in place a recall procedure. The guideline also establishes that, "The parallel importer may use the proprietary name approved in South Africa as well as any trade marks applicable to the medicine in order to ensure the public health interests."

Assume that the procurement authority in South Africa seeks to purchase an anti-infective medicine used to treat opportunistic infections associated with HIV/AIDS and that medicine is under patent in South Africa and Thailand. The anti-infective is sold by the patent holder's authorized distributor in Thailand to wholesale purchasers at $1.00 per capsule. The same anti-infective is sold by the patent holder's authorized distributor in South Africa to wholesale purchasers at $2.50 per capsule. The procurement authority in South Africa can purchase the anti-infective from a wholesaler in Thailand and import it. The patent holder in South Africa will not be able to block the importation based on its local patent because its patent rights are "exhausted" when the medicine is first sold in Thailand.

---

country. The theory behind "nonexhaustion" would be that the patent holder did not "consent" to the sale, and so has not had the chance to exploit the value of the patent. The theory behind "exhaustion" in these circumstances is that the patent holder receives "adequate remuneration" in the exporting country and does in fact receive an economic return. The discussion in this section will be updated as the legal situation surrounding exhaustion and its relationship to compulsory licensing becomes clarified through practice.

tual property rights may not be used to block the importation. Products imported under a rule of international exhaustion are often referred to as "parallel imports." Parallel import medicines are typically purchased from a party other than the patent holder—for example, from a medicine wholesaler that initially purchased from the patent holder in the "first sale." By its first sale to the wholesaler, the patent holder "exhausts" its right to prevent the wholesaler from reselling the medicine and any right of the patent holder to block importation into a country with a rule of international exhaustion.

"Differential" or "equity" pricing refers to selling medicines at lower prices in beneficiary markets while maintaining higher prices for the same medicines in nonbeneficiary markets. It is perceived as a way of allowing innovating companies to recover research and development costs in higher income markets, while making medicines more affordable in lower income markets.

Procurement authorities purchasing and importing medicines under preferential pricing arrangements may be asked by patent holders for contractual commitments not to re-export or permit the re-export of medicines. This is requested so that "arbitragers" will not be allowed to purchase and resell the medicines in wealthier markets, thereby depriving the intended beneficiaries of access to the low-priced medicines and undercutting the economic return from the patent in the wealthier markets. While it is reasonable to provide a contractual commitment not to re-export preferentially priced medicines, the procurement authority should be careful not to make commitments that exceed its internal control capacity. If commitments are made, resources will need to be allocated to fulfilling them.

The law of a developing country should ordinarily permit enforcement of a contract that includes a commitment not to re-export in the same manner as other contractual commitments.

It is sometimes thought that a rule of international exhaustion allowing for parallel imports is inconsistent with preferential pricing of medicines. The suggestion is that patent holders fearing parallel importation of low-price medicines into wealthier markets will refrain from supplying low-price medicines. But rules that prohibit the importation of preferentially priced medicines are already in place in most if not all of the major developed country markets. And if authorities cooperate in preventing the re-export of preferentially priced products, parallel importation should not be an obstacle to preferential pricing arrangements. If this does become a problem, governments may have to increase their cooperative efforts to control the movement of preferentially priced medicines.

### Compulsory licensing and government use

Most or all countries—developed and developing—allow the government to make use of patented inventions for public purposes with fewer bureaucratic obstacles than apply to the private sector. The procurement authority may find it useful to invoke this authority in obtaining HIV/ AIDS medicines. There remains an obligation to pay the patent holder "adequate remuneration in the circumstances of each case, taking into account the economic value of the authorization." The remuneration may be determined after the fact.

To overcome obstacles that may be presented by patents, developing country governments and their procurement authorities can secure access to HIV/AIDS–related medicines, including ARVs, through a "compulsory license" or "government use" authorization. Recall that a patent is a government grant that permits its holder to exclude third parties from the market for a product, such as an HIV/ AIDS-related medicine. A "compulsory license" is an authorization by the government to itself or to a third party to use the patent without the permission of the patent holder. A compulsory license authorizing the government to use the patent for its own purposes is also referred to as a "government use" authorization (in British terminology, "Crown use"). The term "compulsory licensing" is used here to refer to compulsory licensing and government use authorization, unless expressly indicated otherwise.

The legal concept of compulsory licensing is long embedded in international patent law. The patent system involves a tradeoff between the interests of society in encouraging new invention (and disclosure) and the interests of society in promoting competitive markets, access to products, and affordable prices. Since the earliest discussions of an international patent system, it was recognized that governments would encounter circumstances in which social interests in access and affordability would override longer term interests in encouraging invention (by granting exclusive rights to patent holders). It was also recognized that the government would be entitled to use or authorize the use of the patent without the consent of the patent holder. The law of every country allows for some form of compulsory licensing of patents.[22]

Important HIV/AIDS medicines or supplies are covered by one or more patents in many countries. If the procurement authority wishes to procure a bioequivalent medicine (a generic version) from a party other than the patent holder or its authorized distributor, including by importing the medicine, it may need to authorize procurement under a compulsory license. The TRIPS Agreement, in Article 31, authorizes every government to grant compulsory licenses without restriction as to purpose. This authority was confirmed in paragraph 5(b) of the Doha Declaration.[23] Article 31 establishes certain procedural and substantive requirements regarding compulsory licensing. For government procurement authorities dealing with HIV/AIDS medicines, the procedural requirements are minimized in important ways. Note that the procurement authority is not required to use these "fast track" options, and may decide to seek a voluntary license, waiver of enforcement, or price concessions from the patent holder prior to granting a compulsory license. The special rules, in any case, provide assurance that the procurement authority can act rapidly when the situation calls for it.

Under Article 31(b) of the TRIPS Agreement, a party seeking a compulsory license must first have sought a license from the patent holder "on reasonable commercial terms and conditions and [indicate] that such efforts have not been successful within a reasonable period of time." But government procurement authorities do not need to comply with this precondition in respect of HIV/AIDS medicines, on two separate grounds:

First, the precondition may be waived for national emergency or other circumstances of extreme urgency. And the Doha Declaration has expressly recognized that "HIV/AIDS, tuberculosis, malaria and other epidemics, can represent a national emergency or other circumstances of extreme urgency."[24] To take advantage of the right to waive the precondition under these circumstances, the government does not need to

---

[22] We are not aware of any country the law of which does not allow for compulsory licensing or government use in some form. Even if the patent law does not expressly incorporate such a provision, the sovereign authority of the state to take private property for government purposes (with such compensation as may be provided for under constitutional principles) will allow at least for government use.

[23] See text at note 9 above.

[24] Declaration, para. 5(c), note 12 above.

"declare" a general national emergency under legislation or constitutional authority that may allow it to suspend a citizen's rights on a temporary basis. It is legally sufficient that the national health authority state that a compulsory license be granted because of a national health emergency or an extremely urgent public health circumstance. It is highly unlikely that any patent holder or foreign government would seek to challenge the validity of such a statement in the HIV/AIDS context, particularly in view of the Doha Declaration.

Second, the precondition may also be waived "in cases of public non-commercial use." The precise meaning or limit of "public non-commercial use" is not spelled out in the TRIPS Agreement, leaving developing countries to interpret the term in good faith. It is clear, however, that a government procurement authority purchasing HIV/AIDS medicines for distribution through public clinics and without seeking to make a commercial profit from such distribution, will be engaging in "public non-commercial use." If members of the public are required to bear all or a portion of the cost of the medicines either directly or through health insurance, this should not affect the public noncommercial character of the transaction as long as the government was not seeking to profit from the arrangement (that is, if the arrangement is essentially revenue neutral). There may well be further flexibility inherent in the "public non-commercial use" language of the TRIPS Agreement.[25]

The situation for HIV/AIDS is expressly recognized in the Doha Declaration. The HIV/AIDS pandemic is a national emergency and circumstance of extreme urgency in every developing country confronting it. From a practical standpoint, it may be easiest and most efficient for a government and its procurement authority to rely on the ground of national

---

[25] There are many ways that the terms "public non-commercial use" may be defined in good faith. The term "public" could refer to use by a government, as opposed to private entity. The term "public" may refer also to the purpose of the use, that is, use for "public" benefit. A private entity could be charged with exploiting a patent for the benefit of the public.

"Noncommercial use" may be defined either in relation to the nature of the transaction, or in relation to the purpose of the use. On the nature of the transaction, "noncommercial" may be understood as "not-for-profit" use. A commercial enterprise does not ordinarily enter the market without intending to earn a profit. Regarding the purpose of the use, "noncommercial" may refer to the supply of public institutions that are not functioning as commercial enterprises. The supply of a public hospital operating on a nonprofit basis may be a "noncommercial" use of the patent.

"Public noncommercial use" is a flexible concept, leaving governments considerable flexibility in granting compulsory licenses without requiring commercial negotiations in advance.

emergency or extreme urgency as the basis for a waiver under TRIPS Article 31(b). For HIV/AIDS, the ground of public noncommercial use may work just as well in view of the pandemic and urgent need to address it. But if patent holders should fear that the public noncommercial use grounds may be used by procurement authorities "down the road" in more nuanced circumstances, some patent holders might choose to challenge its use even for HIV/AIDS as a "matter of legal principle," thereby inviting delays.

To sum up, a government may issue a compulsory license to its procurement authority to acquire generic HIV/AIDS medicines, including by import, despite the presence of a local patent by stating that it is doing so to address a national emergency or circumstance of extreme urgency. As a matter of general practice, it is preferable that national patent or public health laws or regulations expressly provide a basis for such action. But if such laws or regulations are not in place, this does not prevent a government from taking this action. Inherent in the sovereignty of every government is the right to protect the public interest in a national emergency or circumstance of extreme urgency, and the government does not need to refer to specific national legislation to exercise this authority. Nothing in the TRIPS Agreement requires that the steps a government takes in these circumstances be laid out in advance.

Article 31(h) of the TRIPS Agreement requires that "the right holder shall be paid adequate remuneration in the circumstances of each case, taking into account the economic value of the authorization." The TRIPS Agreement does not attempt to define "adequate remuneration," leaving it to each government to determine this amount in good faith. The government does not need to determine this amount in advance of granting the compulsory license, and its legislation may specifically refuse to allow a patent holder the right to seek an injunction to block the granting of a license for government use.[26]

When a compulsory license is granted for procurement of a generic version of an HIV/AIDS medicine or supply, the government will be dealing with the circumstance of attempting to maximize the quantity of

---

[26] Article 44:2, TRIPS Agreement, provides in relevant part: "Notwithstanding the other provisions of this Part and provided that the provisions of Part II specifically addressing use by governments, or by third parties authorized by a government, without the authorization of the right holder are complied with, Members may limit the remedies available against such use to payment of remuneration in accordance with subparagraph (h) of Article 31."

medicines it can procure, and with the highest level of public interest at stake. Under these circumstances, the government may be justified in limiting "adequate remuneration" to the patent holder to a low royalty based on the purchase price of the generic medicines.

Article 31 of the TRIPS Agreement includes other procedural and substantive requirements for granting compulsory licenses. Because national legislation and regulations have been, or will be, revised to take into account these requirements, the procurement authority should be able to ascertain the requirements of national law. Certainly, however, implementation of the TRIPS Agreement is an ongoing process. And as developing members gain experience, they will be evaluating their laws and regulations to determine whether they adequately account for the public interest.[27]

Government use and compulsory licensing are the principal means enabling procurement authorities to overcome patent barriers to obtaining lower priced generic medicines and related supplies. But for many developing countries the option to use such licensing is illusory. They do not have sufficient local production capacity to make needed medicines at a reasonable cost.[28]

The TRIPS Agreement generally allows WTO members to grant compulsory licenses and to satisfy those licenses by importing. However, there is a catch. There must be medicines lawfully available for import. In other words, even if patent barriers are overcome domestically, there may be patents in prospective exporting countries that prevent the manufacture and export of needed medicines and supplies.[29] This problem will become very serious after January 1, 2005, when all developing countries are required to have patent protection for pharmaceutical products in place, and when "mailbox" pipeline applications that have

––––––––––––––––––

[27] There are a number of published sources that can be consulted for this purpose. The United Nations Conference on Trade and Development and the International Center for Trade and Sustainable Development have developed a TRIPS Resource Book that contains detailed practical information regarding the implementation of the TRIPS Agreement from the perspective of developing countries (available at www.iprsonline.org) The World Health Organization also has important publications on this subject. Available at www.who.int/medicines.

[28] Also, a country without sufficient production capacity may have difficulty making price demands because it lacks a credible threat of taking over production.

[29] This is not an absolute barrier because TRIPS compulsory licensing rules only require that a "predominant" part of production be for domestic supply. So, if there is a substantial domestic market for a generic medicine in an exporting country, and a license has been granted for that market, there may be a significant supply available for export.

accumulated during the past 10 years are given effect.[30] The availability of newer off-patent medicines from India, as the most notable illustration, will be reduced.

The WTO addressed the problem of countries with insufficient or no capacity in the pharmaceutical sector and their inability to make effective use of compulsory licensing in "Paragraph 6" negotiations that concluded on August 30, 2003.[31] The result of these negotiations was a "waiver" of the provision of the TRIPS Agreement that otherwise might limit exports under compulsory license (Article 31(f)).[32] A procuring-importing country (except a least developed country, which is automatically eligible) needs to notify the WTO that it intends to take advantage of the waiver.[33] It may then request that a producer in an exporting country supply it.[34] The producer may be a private enterprise, or it may be the government (or a private enterprise acting on its behalf). The exporting country must grant a license authorizing use of the patent for export. When imports commence there should also be a license in the importing country (if a license is needed to overcome a domestically granted patent).[35]

The waiver also exempts the importing country from an obligation under Article 31(h) of the TRIPS Agreement to pay remuneration since

---

[30] The term of a "mailbox" patent will be based on its initial filing date, so the duration will be shorter than that of a newly applied for patent.

[31] WTO General Council, Implementation of paragraph 6 of the Doha Declaration on the TRIPS Agreement and Public Health, IP/C/W/405, August 30, 2003, and The General Council Chairperson's statement, August 30, 2003 (available at www.wto.org). "Paragraph 6" refers to the paragraph of the Doha Declaration on the TRIPS Agreement and Public Health that provided the mandate for these negotiations.

[32] The "waiver" was adopted without prejudice to other legal rights WTO Members may have. So, for example, if Article 30 that allows exceptions to the rights of patent holders can be used by exporting countries as the basis for exports, this right has not been taken away. It was in part uncertainty concerning how Article 30 will be interpreted by the WTO Appellate Body that led to the Paragraph 6 negotiations. Also, the waiver provides that WTO Members will before the end of 2003 commence working on a formal amendment to the TRIPS Agreement that eventually will be substituted for the waiver. The terms of the amendment should be at least as favorable to procurement authorities as the waiver, so the terms described above should satisfy the TRIPS Agreement under any reasonably foresee able circumstance.

[33] This may be a "one-time" notification. It is not necessary to repeat this notification each time the waiver is used. However, both the importing and the exporting countries must provide further notifications (with respect to the name of the product and certain other matters) whenever the system set out in the August 30, 2003, decision is used.

[34] The exporting country may be a developed or developing country.

[35] A least developed member may decide it will not enforce a patent, and in that case will not need to grant a license. Also, there may not be a patent in force in the importing member.

the patent holder will be compensated in the exporting country "taking into account the economic value to the importing Member of the use that has been authorized in the exporting Member."

The August 30, 2003, decision of the General Council and the accompanying statement of the Chairperson contain further detailed provisions for its implementation.[36] Because the Paragraph 6 solution is new as of August 2003, there will be a start-up period as prospective exporting countries decide on the best way to implement the rules.[37]

## Registration and regulatory review

Medicines are typically registered by public health authorities before they are placed into use. The registration process may include the import of a sample of a generic medicine, and a local patent holder may object to the import for such registration purposes. A WTO member is permitted under Article 30 of the TRIPS Agreement to provide a limited exception to the rights of patent holders to allow third party acts involved in the registration process (a "regulatory review exception"). Such an exception may be adopted by specific legislation or regulation, or the courts may allow such an exception on their own. When the procurement authority acquires generic medicine under a government use or compulsory license, that authorization should in any case allow for registration of the medicine.

The TRIPS Agreement in Article 39.3 includes a requirement that a narrowly defined category of undisclosed test or other data submitted as a condition of marketing approval be protected against "unfair commercial use."[38] The provision applies only to "pharmaceutical or agricultural chemical products that utilize new chemical entities."

---

[36] These provisions are explained in Exportation of Drugs under Compulsory Licenses: The WTO Decision on Implementation of Paragraph 6 of the Doha Declaration on the TRIPS Agreement and Public Health, available at www1.worldbank.org/hiv_aids/docs/GHAPnote10.03.03.pdf.pdf.

[37] Specific implementing legislation is not necessarily required in each prospective exporting country, for example, if its law allows for the direct application of TRIPS rules. It is, however, likely that a number of countries will elect to amend their patent law to implement the waiver.

[38] Article 39, TRIPS Agreement: "3. Members, when requiring, as a condition of approving the marketing of pharmaceutical or of agricultural chemical products, which utilize new chemical entities, the submission of undisclosed test or other data, the origination of which involves a considerable effort, shall protect such data against unfair commercial use. In addition, Members shall protect such data against disclosure, except where necessary to protect the public, or unless steps are taken to ensure that the data are protected against unfair commercial use."

Typically a generic pharmaceutical product, including an HIV/AIDS medicine, will be registered by local public health authorities before it is distributed to the public. It is at this stage that a patent holder may argue that the public health authorities should not be allowed to rely on test data provided by the patent holder, even if submitted by it for approval of the medicine in another country, because to do so would take unfair commercial advantage of its efforts. The patent holder may suggest that a generic producer should be required to generate an entirely new set of test data as a condition of registration, even though doing so would involve delay and duplicate efforts with no corresponding public benefit. Patent holders use data protection claims as aggressively as traditional intellectual property rights claims to attempt to block the introduction of generic medicines.

There is considerable legal controversy over the scope of the obligation that Article 39.3 of the TRIPS Agreement places on WTO members. It is clear, however, that claims to protection of data and claims to patent protection are different matters. The fact that there is a patent on a medicine does not preclude its registration as a generic.[39] Developing country governments should include a regulatory review exception in their approach to patents. Developing country governments should make suitable provisions in their regulatory frameworks to facilitate registration when data are used for public purposes. When a government is approving the use of a medicine for HIV/AIDS treatment in its health care system, it is not making "unfair commercial use" of originator data. It is addressing an urgent public health need.[40]

## Determining the patent status of HIV/AIDS medicines

To determine whether government authorization to import a generic HIV/AIDS medicine or supply medicine is required, the procurement authority needs to check whether that medicine is locally under patent in-

---

[39] This was confirmed by a WTO dispute settlement panel in Canada—Patent Protection of Pharmaceutical Products, WT/DS114/R, March 17, 2000. The potential inhibiting effects of patents on medicines registration can be avoided by use of a regulatory review exception, or by authorizing acts in connection with registration in a government use or compulsory license.

[40] For a thoughtful discussion of this topic, see U.K. Commission on Intellectual Property Rights, Integrating Intellectual Property Rights and Development Policy, at 50–51 (Report of the Commission on Intellectual Property Rights, London, 2002).

country. The relevant branded medicine may not be available locally, with patent numbers listed on an information sheet, to readily indicate the situation in the local market.[41] Unfortunately, the procedure for determining whether a particular medicine is under patent is often difficult. Patents are not granted or listed by categories that allow for searches according to trademark, brand name, international nonproprietary name, or other medicinal classification. Often a medicine that is well known under a trademark or brand name will be protected by several linked patents, and the links will not be identified in a single patent disclosure. Pharmaceutical patent holders are not always anxious to allow their competitors to determine whether a particular molecule or formulation technology is covered by patent.

Persons who are not specialists in the technology of pharmaceuticals will find it difficult to determine the patent status of a particular medicine by, for example, examining published patents. One possible route for the procurement authority is to make a request to the national patent office to provide a report on which HIV/AIDS medicines are under patent locally and the period of patent protection. But not all national patent offices are willing or prepared to undertake this activity. Another possible method is to engage the services of a professional patent-searching firm that will prepare a report for a fee. Depending upon the complexity of the search, the fee may be substantial.

Responding to the difficulties created by this situation, some nongovernmental organizations, notably Médecins Sans Frontières, have been working for several years to identify the patent situation of HIV/AIDS medicines in developing countries. It is publishing and updating lists describing the patent situation in a number of countries. But it cautions that it cannot provide information with absolute certainty for the technical reasons described above. It may not be possible to state with certainty that all of the patents linked to a particular medicine have been identified. Even so, until improvements in this situation are agreed on at the international level, the best information available may be obtained from Médecins Sans Frontières. More work is needed on identifying patents associated with medicines. This will require cooperation among public

---

[41] When a producer lists a patent number on medicines packaging, this should indicate that the producer holds or is the licensee of the relevant patent. But this does not mean that the patent is valid, and many patents challenged in courts or administrative tribunals are found to be invalid.

health organizations, such as the World Health Organization, along with national and regional offices maintaining patent data.

## Trademarks and copyrights

The producer of generic HIV/AIDS medicine or supplies will typically avoid using the trademark or brand name of another producer, because this invites costly litigation. It is therefore unlikely that procurement authorities will find it necessary to be concerned with potential claims for trademark infringement. However, there are two possibilities to which attention should be drawn.

First, branded pharmaceuticals producers sometimes assert that the color or shape of medicine is protected as their trademark. This area of trademark law also involves a degree of controversy. Although colors may serve as trademarks, when a color serves a useful (or utilitarian) function, it is not serving as a trademark, but as an idea or method of use. If physicians, pharmacists, and patients associate a particular kind of drug with a particular color, the color serves a function allowing easy identification for health-related purposes. Very frequently, patients come to rely on the color and shape of a drug as a primary means of identification. For this reason, a developing country can defend the introduction of a comparably colored or shaped medicine on grounds that the color and shape serve a functional, as contrasted with a trademark, purpose. Moreover, Article 17 of the TRIPS Agreement allows for the limited "fair use" of trademarks, and it is certainly in the fair public interest to allow the use of colors in generic medicines when purchased and distributed by public health authorities. It is nonetheless useful to be aware of the possibility of such claims.

Second, recall the earlier discussion of parallel importation. The seller of a medicine trademarked in one country may also seek to block importation of the medicine into another country based on the independent registration of its mark. If the government permits parallel importation, the authorization should also extend to trademarks and copyrights because these intellectual property rights are also invoked by medicines producers to attempt to block the introduction of generics. Even when purchasing directly from the trademark holder or authorized distributor in an exporting country, the importing procurement authority should obtain acknowledgement that intellectual property rights will not be invoked to block importation. A court may well decide that such authorization is an implied condition of the sale, but it is wise to avoid such complications.

Legislation and regulations in a developing member should also address the possibility that an HIV/AIDS medicine producer will assert copyright interests in physician or patient information materials. Copyright interests are subject to "fair use" under the TRIPS Agreement, Article 13, with cross reference to Berne Convention Article 9(2). When HIV/AIDS-related generic medicines are procured by public health authorities, this will constitute fair use of information materials, which in any case are not likely to be considered "expressive works" within the meaning of copyright.

ANNEX

# C

## HIV Test Kits and Other Diagnostics

When used correctly, HIV tests can determine if HIV is present in a person's blood. There are two main types of HIV tests:

- Antibody tests, such as ELISA, simple-rapid, and Western blot.
- Virologic tests, such as the HIV antigen test, polymerase chain reaction test, and viral culture.

## Antibody tests

HIV antibody tests look for antibodies against HIV; they do not detect the virus itself. When HIV enters the body, it infects white blood cells known as T4 lymphocytes, or CD4 cells. The infected person's immune system responds by producing antibodies to fight the new HIV infection. The presence of the antibodies is used to determine the presence of HIV infection. Enzyme immunoassays (EIAs) are recommended for laboratories that process large numbers of specimens daily. Rapid tests are useful in settings where EIAs are not practical and in geographic areas with limited laboratory infrastructure. The Western blot is used mainly to confirm a prior test.

## Virologic tests

Antibody tests are the most commonly used tests, but under special circumstances—in a recently infected individual, during the window period, or for a child born to an HIV-positive mother—more direct diagnostic methods may be used. Unlike antibody tests, virologic tests determine HIV infection by detecting the virus itself. Virologic tests are rarely used to diagnose HIV in developing countries since they require sophisticated laboratories. But they may be used to monitor progress of infection or response to therapy, say by measuring viral load.

HIV testing strategies vary from one country to the other depending on the estimated HIV prevalence and available technologies. Ordinarily, it is the responsibility of government regulatory bodies—ministries of health, national HIV/AIDS control programs, or national reference laboratories—to formulate the most feasible testing strategies for a country.

UNAIDS/WHO recommend using two or three different combinations of EIAs or rapid tests as a testing strategy. The first test, a screening test, should be highly sensitive to reliably detect antibodies. The second test, a confirmatory test, should be highly specific to confirm that the specimen truly contains antibodies specific to HIV.

Factors to consider in developing an HIV testing strategy include:

- Expected HIV prevalence
- Laboratory infrastructure
- Availability of refrigerators/regular electricity
- Performance of test kits
- Cost
- Impact on the delivery of health services.

Testing strategies should be designed to maximize both sensitivity and specificity for HIV antibody detection.

## Selecting HIV test kits

The selected test kits should have been evaluated by WHO and meet the requirements of at least 99 percent sensitivity and at least 99 percent specificity.[1]

---

[1] UNAIDS/WHO. Operational Characteristics of Commercially Available Assays to Determine Antibodies to HIV-1 and/or HIV-2 in Human Sera. Reports 11, 12 and 13. Geneva: UNAIDS/WHO.

In addition to the performance of the HIV test kits, various operational factors influence the selection of assays:

- Laboratory infrastructure
- Access to a reference laboratory
- Desired characteristics of the test (antigen, antibody)
- Simplicity of test procedure
- Equipment necessary to perform the test
- Performance time
- Shelf life of reagents
- Price
- Storage conditions
- Technical skill of laboratory staff
- Laboratory logistics.

Countries should evaluate the accuracy and operational characteristics of HIV test kits in-country and determine the most appropriate combination and sequence of tests. While most countries will already have a national testing strategy, many may not have the capacity to evaluate test kits in-country.

If the national laboratory infrastructure lacks the capacity to perform the evaluation, then after selecting a test(s) from the UNAIDS/WHO list, a testing algorithm can be chosen based on evaluations by another independent, noncommercial source, preferably in the region.

For more detailed information on selecting a HIV testing strategy and selecting HIV test kits, please see the following:

- UNAIDS/WHO (1999). Operational characteristics of commercially available assays to determine antibodies to HIV-1 and/or HIV-2 in human sera. Reports 11, 12 and 13. Geneva: UNAIDS/WHO or visit www.who.int/bct/Main_areas_of_work/BTS/ HIV_Diagnostics/HIV_Test_Kit_Evaluation.htm (Note: Addresses of manufacturers are also included at the back of these reports.)
- WHO/CDC/UNAIDS (2001) Guidelines for using HIV testing technologies in surveillance, evaluation and implementation. Geneva: UNAIDS/WHO.
- Walkowiak, H. and Gabra, M. (2002). Commodity Management in VCT Programs: A planning guide. Management Sciences for Health

(RPM Plus) and Family Health International or visit www.msh.org/ resources/online_reports/pdf/VCT_Final.pdf

Countries should require that all laboratories (national, regional, and local) that conduct HIV testing, participate in an external quality assurance of a laboratory's procedure. In addition, they should have a functioning internal quality assurance program. All laboratories should routinely monitor and assess the quality in the preanalytical, analytical, and postanalytical phases of the testing. Details of the components to be monitored in each phase can be found in "Guidelines for Using HIV Testing Technologies in Surveillance."[2]

## Quantification

Before procuring HIV test kits, countries must decide how many kits and other commodities to buy. Some manufacturers and suppliers will help providers quantify their needs (on the basis of the experience with other countries and facilities) and establish delivery schedules.

HIV test kits are complicated products to manage. First, their average shelf life is a short 12 months, requiring smaller and more frequent shipments. Second, many of the kits require cold storage, limiting the number of locations where they can be stored. Third, use can vary greatly between service delivery points within a single country. And fourth, few data exist for logistics and consumption in large programs, complicating the accurate forecasting of demand.

## General principles for quantification

- Use at least two quantification methods to check your estimates.
- When quantifying needs for a new service or intervention, order extra supplies to "fill the pipeline."
- Quantification will need to consider lead time—the average time between recognizing that a commodity needs to be ordered to having it available for use. The longer the lead time is, the more safety or buffer stock will be needed to prevent stockouts between orders.

---

[2] UNAIDS/WHO *Guidelines for Using HIV Testing Technologies in Surveillance.* 2001. Geneva: UNAIDS/WHO.

■ Adjust quantification estimates for losses or waste, and take into account the amount of products already in the system.

■ No matter which method is used, there is usually a gap between estimated needs and available funds, and decisions will need to be made on how to adjust and reconcile the quantities needed.

Source: Walkowiak, H., and M. Gabra. VCT Toolkit: Commodity Management in VCT Programs: A Planning Guide. Family Health International/Management Sciences for Health, December 2002.

## Procurement

Whichever procurement source used, all HIV test kits must have been evaluated by WHO and meet the requirements of at least 99% sensitivity and at least 99% specificity.

Test kits can be purchased using one of the following procurement options:[3]

■ WHO bulk HIV test kit procurement scheme
■ Limited international bidding
■ Direct contracting or shopping

WHO established the HIV Test Kit Bulk Procurement Scheme in 1989. The goals of the scheme are to facilitate access to high-quality test kits at a low cost through an easy purchase procedure.

There are 22 tests on the WHO Current Bulk Procurement Scheme List of Available Assays, including a greater number of simple-rapid assays than ever before. This scheme encompasses the main types of tests used to detect HIV antibodies today—EIAs, simple-rapid assays, and confirmatory assays. WHO negotiates prices for all assays in the bulk procurement scheme directly with the manufacturers, enabling it to offer a per test cost of about half that of the open market price.

After selecting HIV test kits that have been evaluated by WHO and meet the minimum requirements for specificity and sensitivity, kits may be procured from a limited number of sources through competition.

---

[3] Market information (e.g., names of manufacturers and prices) that can be used to help countries make informed decisions is included in MSF/UNICEF/UNAIDS/WHO's publication: "Sources and Prices of Selected Medicines and Diagnostics for People Living with HIV/AIDS/ June 2003."

## Ancillary equipment and supplies

In addition to HIV test kits, the consumables needed for HIV testing may include the following:

- Automated analyzers, such as ELISA readers
- Reagents and controls for ELISA testing (if appropriate to the quality assurance strategy)
- Centrifuges
- Refrigerators
- Test tube racks
- Timers
- Consumables, such as pipettes, pipette tips, and specimen tubes
- Supplies to collect specimens, such as lancets, needles, syringes and plasters
- Disposable gloves
- Disinfectants and cleaning supplies
- Sharps disposal bins for needles and lancets as defined under the Universal Precautions strategy
- Waste disposal (biohazard) bags for blood-contaminated non-sharps, such as gauze, swabs, gloves, and testing cards.

Increased access to ARVs has also highlighted the need for appropriate and cost-effective diagnostic support. Diagnostic support is essential to monitor the progression of the disease, the effectiveness of treatment, and the development of resistance. The main measures used are CD4+/CD8+ cell counts and viral loads.

Accurate and reliable measures of CD4+/CD8+ cells help in assessing the immune system and managing the health care of persons infected with HIV. The pathogenesis of AIDS is largely attributable to the decrease in the number of CD4+/CD8+ cells. Progressive depletion is associated with an increased likelihood of severe HIV disease.

The most common method to measure CD4+/CD8+ cells is multi-platform or single-platform flow cytometry. But this is also the most complicated and expensive method. Several alternative methods require fewer reagents and may be more cost-effective.

Using highly active antiretroviral therapy (HAART) and monitoring therapy response by using viral load testing have contributed to clinical management of persons infected with HIV. Measurements of viral load can be used to determine when ART should be initiated and to monitor treatment efficacy.

The most commonly used viral load assays are nucleic acid based. Of these, only three have been approved by the U.S. Food and Drug Administration (FDA) which means that they have undergone extensive evaluation.

- The HIV-1 reverse transcriptase polymerase chain reaction assay (Amplicor HIV-1 Monitor Test, version 1.5, Roche Diagnostic),
- In vitro nucleic amplification test for HIV-RNA (NucliSens HIV-1 QT, by Organon Tekniak),
- In vitro signal amplification nucleic acid probe assay (VERSANT HIV-1 RNA 3.0 Assay.[4]

Other types of nucleic acid and nonnucleic acid viral load assays may perform equally well. To make a decision about which viral load assay to use, review the information in the MSF guide.[5]

---

[4] Centers for Disease Control and Prevention. (November 16, 2001). Guidelines for Laboratory Test Result Reporting of Human Immunodeficiency Virus Type 1 Ribonucleic Acid Determination. *MMWR* November 16, 2001/Vol.50/No. RR-20.
[5] MSF/UNICEF/UNAIDS/WHO. Sources and Prices of Selected Medicines and Diagnostics for People Living with HIV/AIDS. June, 2003.

# *Glossary*

The terms listed below are defined specifically for the purposes of this Guide. They may be defined differently in other documentation, including referenced documents and annexes, which were, in certain cases, published some years ago.

**Adherence.** Compliance with treatment; strictly following the drug regimen.

**Accountability.** Being required to account for one's conduct and actions, usually to an individual or group but ultimately to the public. Both individuals and organizations may be accountable. There is some overlap between accountability and *transparency*.

**Active pharmaceutical ingredient.** A substance or compound that is intended to be used in the manufacture of a pharmaceutical product as a therapeutically active compound (ingredient).

**ARVs.** Antiretroviral drugs, used for treating symptoms related to AIDS.

**Bioequivalence.** Two pharmaceutical products are bioequivalent if they are pharmaceutically equivalent and their bioavailabilities (rate and extent of availability), after administration in the same molar dose, are similar to such a degree that their effects can be expected to be essentially the same.

**CD4 Test.**  A test to measure the CD4+ cell count—a vital measure of the state of a person's immune system. According to the Center for Disease Control and Prevention, any person who has a CD4+ count of lower than 200 has AIDS.

**Compulsory licensing.**  An authorization by the government to itself or to a third party to use a patent without the permission of the patent holder. A compulsory license authorizing the government to use the patent for its own purposes is also referred to as a "government use" authorization (in British terminology, "Crown use"). The term "compulsory licensing" is used in this report to refer to compulsory licensing and government use authorization, unless expressly indicated otherwise.

**Container labelling.**  All information that appears on any part of a container, including that on any outer packaging such as a carton.

**Differential pricing.**  Sometimes called "equity pricing," or tiered pricing, this is a system whereby medicines are sold at prices that relate to the income of consumers. In rich countries, prices will be higher, in poor countries, prices will be lower.

**Dosage form.**  The form of the completed pharmaceutical product—for example, a tablet, capsule, injection, elixir, or suppository.

**Drug.**  Any substance or pharmaceutical product for human or veterinary use that is intended to modify or explore physiological systems or pathological states for the benefit of the recipient.

**Drug product.**  *See* pharmaceutical product.

**Drug regulatory authority (national).**  A national body that administers the full spectrum of drug regulatory activities, including at least the following functions:

- Marketing authorization of new products and variation of existing products
- Quality control laboratory testing
- Adverse drug reaction monitoring
- Provision of drug information and promotion of rational drug use
- Good manufacturing practice inspections and licensing of manufacturers, wholesalers, and distribution channels

- Enforcement operations
- Monitoring of drug utilization.

**Equity pricing.** *See* differential pricing.

**Essential drugs.** Drugs that satisfy the health care needs of the majority of the population. As indicated by the Expert Committee on the Use of Essential Drugs, each country may generate its own list of essential drugs.

**Evaluation report.** A critical summary and interpretation of the data, with conclusions, prepared by or on behalf of the drug regulatory authority.

**Excipient.** Any component of a finished dosage form other than the claimed therapeutic ingredient or ingredients.

**Finished product.** A product that has undergone all stages of production, including packaging in its final container and labelling.

**Formulation.** The composition of a dosage form, including the characteristics of its raw materials and the operations required to process it.

**Generic products.** The term "generic product" has somewhat different meanings in different contexts. *Generic product* and *multisource pharmaceutical product* (see below) are terms used interchangeably. Generic products may be marketed either under the approved international non-proprietary name or under a brand (proprietary) name. They may be marketed in dosage forms and/or strengths different from those of the innovator products. Where the term generic product is used, it means a pharmaceutical product, usually intended to be interchangeable with the innovator product, which is usually manufactured without a licence from the innovator company and marketed after expiration of the patent (or under an exception to patent rights) or other exclusive rights. The term should not be confused with generic names for active pharmaceutical ingredients. *Generic* can also be used in a more limited sense of off patent.

**Grandfathered.** A product that is grandfathered is one that has been granted marketing authorization because it was already being marketed at the time the marketing authorization system was established. The terms "provisional registration" or "provisional marketing authorization" are preferred, but some countries do not have a separate category of provisional marketing authorization.

**Intellectual property rights.** Intellectual property rights include patents, trademarks, copyrights, and rights in data assembled for regulatory purposes (rights in data are not strictly "intellectual property"). HIV/AIDS medicines may be subject to claims based on any of these rights, which may affect medicine procurement in different ways.

**Interchangeability.** An interchangeable pharmaceutical product is one that is therapeutically equivalent to a comparator (reference) product.

**Labelling.** The word "labelling" has been avoided in this manual because its meaning is not consistent between Member states. See *container labelling* and *product information.*

**Licence.** *See* registration.

**Limited-source pharmaceutical products.** Drugs available from only a few manufacturers.

**Manufacture.** All operations of purchase of materials and products, production, quality control, release, storage, shipment of finished products and the related controls.

**Marketing authorization.** *See* registration.

**Medicine.** *See* drug.

**Medicinal product.** *See pharmaceutical product.*

**Multisource (generic) pharmaceutical product.** Pharmaceutically equivalent products that may or may not be therapeutically equivalent. Multisource pharmaceutical products that are therapeutically equivalent are interchangeable.

**New drug.** Any drug that does not match the definition of *well-established drugs* (see below).

**Originator or innovator pharmaceutical product.** The first product authorized for marketing (normally as a patented product) on the basis of documentation of efficacy, safety, and quality (according to requirements at the time of the authorization). When a substance has been available for many years, it may not be possible to identify an innovator pharmaceutical product.

**Parallel importation.** The purchase of a patented medicine from a lawful source in an exporting country and its importation without seeking the consent of the "parallel" patent holder in the importing country. The sale of the patented medicine in the exporting country is deemed to "exhaust" the patent holder's right in the importing country.

**Patent.** Granted to the inventor of a product or process giving the inventor the right to exclude others from making, using, selling, offering for sale, and importing[1] a product covered by a product patent, and from using a process covered by a process patent.[2] Patents are granted on a country-to-country basis, and sometimes on a regional basis.

**Periodic review.** The regular process, usually occurring every five years, by which the validity of a marketing authorization is renewed and information on a product is reviewed (validated), consolidated, and sometimes expanded.

**Pharmaceutical equivalents.** Products that contain the same amount of the same active substance(s) in the same dosage form, that meet the same or comparable standards, and that are intended to be administered by the same route. Pharmaceutical equivalence does not necessarily imply therapeutic equivalence, as differences in the excipients or the manufacturing process can lead to differences in product performance.

**Pharmaceutical product.** Any preparation for human or veterinary use that is intended to modify or explore physiological systems or pathological states for the benefit of the recipient.

**Pooled procurement.** Several procurers pooling their buying needs through one source. It can work either nationally (many health systems together) or internationally (many countries together). It is often used when there is either low-volume need or insufficient capacity to procure.

**Prequalification.** A system whereby specific products of a specific pharmaceutical or medical company, or laboratory (in this context), may be

---

[1] The right to prevent importation does not prevent "parallel importation" of a patented medicine when a rule of international exhaustion of patent rights is followed. See chapter 2.

[2] A patent is also used to exclude others from using, selling, offering for sale, and importing a product produced by a patented process.

certified for quality. For example, the WHO certifies a range of pharmaceutical manufacturers for ARVs.

**Procurement.** In this context, the act of buying medicines and related products.

**Product information.** A document defining information that may be supplied with or about a pharmaceutical product by or on behalf of the marketing authorization holder. The minimum information in the product information is that defined by the WHO's sample product information sheet. The content of the product information is agreed between the marketing authorization holder and the drug regulatory authority at the time the market authorization is issued.

**Product selection.** The act of choosing the correct regimen of medicines and related products for a particular health problem.

**Quality control.** Sampling, specifications, and testing, and the organization, documentation, and acceptance and rejection procedures that ensure that the necessary and relevant tests are completed, and that starting materials, intermediates, and finished products are not accepted for use, sale, or supply until their quality has been judged to be satisfactory.

**Quantification.** Establishing the quantity of medicines to be procured for any given health problem.

**Register.** A list of all the pharmaceutical products authorized for marketing in a particular country. The register is maintained by the drug regulatory authority of the country in question.

**Registered drug products.** Pharmaceutical products that have a marketing authorization.

**Registration.** An official document issued by the competent drug regulatory authority for the purpose of marketing or free distribution of a product after evaluation for safety, efficacy, and quality. It must set out, *inter alia*, the name of the product, the pharmaceutical dosage form, the quantitative formula (including excipients) per unit dose (using international nonproprietary or national generic names where they exist), the shelf life and storage conditions, and packaging characteristics. It specifies the information on which authorization is based (for example, "The product(s) must conform with all the details provided in your application and as modified in subsequent correspondence"). It also contains the product information approved for health professionals and the public, the sales category, the name and address of the holder of the authorization, and the period of validity of the authorization. Once a product has been given marketing authorization, it is included on a list of authorized products (the register) and is often said to be "registered" or to "have registration." Marketing authorization may occasionally also be referred to as a licence or product licence.

**Single-source pharmaceutical product.**  A pharmaceutical product only available from one source (the originator). Usually, the product is protected by a patent, and is very new (that is, generic versions are not yet available).

**Specification—expiry, check, or shelf life.**  The combination of physical, chemical, biological, and microbiological test requirements that an active ingredient must meet up to its retest date or a drug product must meet during its shelf life.

**Specification—release.**  The combination of physical, chemical, biological, and microbiological test requirements that determine whether a drug product is suitable for release at the time of its manufacture.

**Stability.**  The ability of an active ingredient or a drug product to retain its properties within specified limits throughout its shelf life. The chemical, physical, microbiological, and biopharmaceutical aspects of stability must be considered.

**Starting material.**  Any substance of a defined quality used in the production of a pharmaceutical product, excluding packaging materials.

**Therapeutic equivalence.**  Two pharmaceutical products are therapeutically equivalent if they are pharmaceutically equivalent and, after administration in the same molar dose, their effects with respect to both efficacy and safety are essentially the same, as determined from appropriate bioequivalence, pharmacodynamic, clinical, or *in vitro* studies.

**Unregistered drug products.**  Pharmaceutical products that do not have a marketing authorization.

**Validation.** The demonstration, with documentary evidence, that any procedure, process, equipment, material, activity, or system actually leads to the expected results.

**Viral load test.** A test establishing the amount of HIV virus in a person's blood.

**Well-established drugs.** Usually active pharmaceutical ingredients (not products) that:

- Have been marketed for at least five years in countries that undertake active postmarketing monitoring.
- Have been widely used in a sufficiently large number of patients to permit the assumption that safety and efficacy are well known.
- Have the same route of administration and strength, and the same or similar indications as in those countries.

Because this definition refers to active pharmaceutical ingredients and not products, it does not take into account possible sensitivities to excipients and other factors that are relevant to therapeutic equivalence.

**Well-established drug products.** Pharmaceutical products that contain well-established drugs that:

- Have been marketed for at least five years in countries that undertake active post-marketing monitoring.
- Have been widely used in a sufficiently large number of patients to permit the assumption that safety and efficacy are well known.
- Have the same route of administration and strength, and the same or similar indications as in those countries.

**WHO-type certificate.** A certificate of pharmaceutical product of the type defined in the World Health Organization Certification Scheme on the Quality of Pharmaceutical Products Moving in International Commerce.

# Index

In this index *f* denotes figure, *t* denotes table, and *n* denotes note.